LINGUISTIC
CHANGE

LINGUISTIC CHANGE

AN INTRODUCTION TO THE HISTORICAL STUDY OF LANGUAGE

By

E. H. STURTEVANT

with a new Introduction by

ERIC P. HAMP

PHOENIX BOOKS

THE
UNIVERSITY
OF
CHICAGO
PRESS

THE UNIVERSITY OF CHICAGO PRESS, CHICAGO & LONDON
The University of Toronto Press, Toronto 5, Canada

Copyright 1917 by The University of Chicago. Published 1917.
First Phoenix Edition 1961. Second Impression 1962. Composed
and printed by THE UNIVERSITY OF CHICAGO PRESS, Chicago,
Illinois, U.S.A.

INTRODUCTION

A slender book should scarcely have a long introduction. A good book surely needs no introduction. To write an introduction to a well-known book verges on insolence.

Science moves at a relentless pace, and in the past century-and-a-half that linguistics has belonged to the fields of knowledge properly called scientific it has proved no exception. Edgar Howard Sturtevant (1875–1952)[1] was a learned and enthusiastic lifelong contributor both to that science and to the bold and lively spirit that has led to its remarkable flowering in America in the past quarter-century. For many prominent American linguists now active Sturtevant was a revered figure, whose staunch and outspoken espousal of the cause of linguistics was an inspiration and whose linguistic books are old friends. It is an irony of the swift pace of science (and of the accidents of printing) that a whole generation of active younger linguists has now come of age to whom Sturtevant's admirable little book *Linguistic Change* is probably nothing more than a bibliographic title at best.

Yet Sturtevant, who fought so hard for the dignity of this thriving discipline that younger scholars take for granted, would cheerfully have had it this way. He always welcomed selflessly the advance of the field as a whole. In his last years he sat down to write a fresh version of his Hittite grammar, unflinchingly rejecting and modifying views that he had defended stoutly and earnestly in former years.

This book is quite out of date—that would no doubt have

---

[1] See *Language*, XXVIII (1952), 417–28, for obituary.

been Sturtevant's first reaction if he could have been con-
sulted today. And in an important sense that is so.[2] But if
one were to dismiss the book at that, one would be over-
looking another implication of the rapid advance of our
science: Sturtevant knew all about the views and outlook
that he wrote about, for he had lived through them. It is
easy for linguists currently being trained to be quite unaware of this significant aspect of the formation of their
chosen field. It is even easier for them to miss entirely a
chance to savor the climate of those times—a delight in
itself.

One might object that there exist fuller and more detailed
sourcebooks of the time, if the history of linguistic theory
is the point in view; Sturtevant himself states in his Preface
that "he is under obligation at some point or many to most
of the standard works on linguistics."[3] But it is wasteful for
more than a few to attempt to recapitulate *in extenso* the
history of their science, and that is not the point here. A
great virtue of this book—apart from those enduringly correct aspects of its doctrine—lies in the fact that in so short
a space the reader may get an accurate impression of the
state of knowledge just before the theoretical outlook now
current in linguistics started to burst upon the field.

The triumph of the nineteenth century—and the beginnings of modern scientific linguistics—was the observation
of the regularity of linguistic change through the elaboration

---

[2] We may profitably compare his later views set forth in *An Introduction
to Linguistic Science* (New Haven, 1947; now available in a paperbound edition, 1960), abbr. *Introduction*.

[3] These would include, besides the classic Indo-European reference works
and monographs of the time, such books as are recommended by Leonard
Bloomfield, *An Introduction to the Study of Language* (New York, [1914]),
pp. 313–18.

of its corollary: the recovery of prehistoric linguistic systems by the use of what came to be known as the comparative method. Sturtevant had a distinguished scholarly ancestry in this regard. He was a pupil of Carl Darling Buck, who was himself a student both of William Dwight Whitney, surely the most lasting great American name from the nineteenth century, and of Karl Brugmann of Leipzig, author of the monumental distillation of nineteenth-century comparative Indo-European knowledge. A convenient survey of this phase of the history of linguistics is to be found in Holger Pedersen's *Linguistic Science in the Nineteenth Century*, translated by John Webster Spargo.

At the turn of the twentieth century the field of systematic dialect geography opened up, largely through the work of the French scholar Jules Gilliéron; and Sturtevant, writing in 1917, was able to integrate some of these findings in his views.[4] He could scarcely, however, have been expected to take into account the seminal doctrines of Saussure on such issues as synchronic versus diachronic linguistics, which were just finding their way into print at that time. Moreover, Sapir, whose imaginative approach was to become so influential, was then just making available his first synthesis of comparative Uto-Aztecan—but this appeared in published channels normally seen by anthropologists rather than by philologists. Indeed, the findings of the anthropologically inspired American Indian researches of Franz Boas and his students (of whom Sapir was certainly the most brilliant) were still largely in the form of synchronic and phonetic descriptions, and their impact for subjects

---

[4] For an exposition taking prominent account of such notions, see W. v. Wartburg, *Problèmes et méthodes de la linguistique* (Paris, 1946), chap. 2, pp. 15–122.

such as concern Sturtevant was yet to come. The fundamental and rigorous comparative Algonquian studies of
Bloomfield still lay in the future.[5]

In the future, too, lay the whole gamut of linguistic theory
now glibly labeled "structural," and attached to such names
as Sapir, Troubetzkoy, Bloomfield, and Hjelmslev. We
might even recall that certain less fortunate views (e.g.,
those of the Italian Bàrtoli and of the Soviet theorist Marr)
had not yet entered the stage to call forth acerb debate at
times—debate that has in any event served to clarify our
grasp of certain fundamental issues. Finally, we should remember that it is only in very recent years that the fruits
of structuralism as applied to diachronic linguistics have
been summarized by André Martinet in his *Économie des
changements phonétiques* (1955) and Henry M. Hoenigswald
in his *Language Change and Linguistic Reconstruction*
(1960).[6]

Let us consider briefly where the main topics of the book
fit in this developmental flow of theory. In the first chapter
the discussions of the distinction of speech and writing, of
the arbitrariness of form in relation to meaning (pp. 23–24),
and of imitation as a source of conservation and conservatism in language (pp. 24–29) remain as fresh as when they

[5] For an appreciation, see C. F. Hockett, "Implications of Bloomfield's
Algonquian Studies," *Language*, XXIV (1948), 117–31.

[6] These are the most extensive, explicit full-length treatments. A recent
briefer textbook exposition is to be found in C. F. Hockett, *A Course in
Modern Linguistics* (New York, 1958), chaps. 41–42, 44–54. However, one
should not overlook the important pioneering essay by Roman Jakobson on
principles of historical phonology (1931), now reprinted in a revised translation in J. Cantineau (trans.), *Principes de phonologie* (Paris, 1949), pp. 315–
36. For an informed and eclectic discussion of Sturtevant's topic, see also
E. Coseriu, *Sincronía, diacronía e historia: El problema del cambio lingüístico*
(Montevideo, 1958).

were written. The brief treatments of alphabets[7] and phonetics stand lucid and serviceable in the main, despite the expectable refinement that these fields have undergone in the intervening years—and, of course, any treatment of phonetics in 1917 would fail to clarify things that the field of phonemics has meantime shed light on.[8] The section on the analysis of language, the area that has seen spectacular development since 1920, is still trenchant, if dated.

In the chapter on primary change of form, the doctrine of lapses has become particularly associated with Sturtevant's name. Linguistic theory of recent decades has rarely touched on the questions dealt with under the rubrics of association (pp. 37–38 and 44 ff.) and analogy;[9] perhaps the growing field of psycholinguistics will have something to say on this score. It is interesting to note that the discussion of rhythm, speed, and ease of utterance is all based on a consideration of purely physical properties, with no mention of the role of structural oppositions such as we should expect today.

The chapter on secondary change of form contains an excellent brief exposition (pp. 70, 72 ff.) of Lautgesetz. In the consideration of isolated changes (pp. 82 ff.), lack of phonemic theory deprived Sturtevant of the possibility of

[7] Cf., too, *Introduction*, pp. 19–29.

[8] See, e.g., *Introduction*, pp. 9 ff.

[9] On analogy one should compare *Introduction*, chap. 10. Eduard Hermann's *Lautgesetz und Analogie* (Berlin, 1931) should not be read apart from Bloomfield's review, *Language*, VIII (1932), 220–33. The most serious recent attempt to systematize analogy in light of modern theory is that of J. Kuryłowicz, "La nature des procès dits 'analogiques,'" *Acta linguistica*, V (1949), 15–37, reprinted in *Esquisses linguistiques* (Wrocław-Kraków, 1960), pp. 66–86. Dissimilation (pp. 52 ff.) has recently been discussed with sophistication, on the basis of rich collections and literature, by Rebecca R. Posner, *Consonantal Dissimilation in the Romance Languages* (Oxford, 1961).

distinguishing these essentially saltatory happenings from regular and gradual (if quantizable) allophonic drifts and mergers.[10]

The chapters on change of meaning and vocabulary remain unsuperseded in essence,[11] although interim developments in anthropological linguistics have revised the language-and-culture notions reflected on pages 105–7; and likewise have trends in modern descriptive analysis departed from the view of composition[12] set forth on pages 110–13. Remarking (p. 131) that there is no clear line of division between syntax and other parts of grammar, Sturtevant is led to treat change in syntax as an extension of his earlier discussion; this view is remarkably in·tune with the convictions of a number of current theorists. Similarly, Sturtevant's healthy remarks (pp. 97–98) on the limits of use for etymology are arrestingly modern and forward-looking in tone.

The treatment of dialect as a unity of sounds perceived (p. 146), of variation in space (pp. 147 ff.), and of larger communities (pp. 155 ff.) is in the main eminently sound, though, to be sure, greater accuracy and finesse have been reached in more recent specialized work. There are, however, two assertions in these passages that stand out as unacceptable today: No one now believes in mixed languages

[10] See now *Introduction*, pp. 76–77.

[11] Cf. *Introduction*, pp. 123–41. Also A. Meillet, "Comment les mots changent de sens," *Linguistique historique et linguistique générale*, I (2d ed., 1926), 230–71; M. B. Emeneau, "Taboos on Animal Names," *Language*, XXIV (1948), 56–63. Of course, on the question of change of vocabulary we find no mention in these works of the recently elaborated subject of lexico-statistics, now under lively discussion in the pages of the journal *Current Anthropology* and elsewhere.

[12] Cf. *Introduction*, p. 129.

or dialects as such (p. 152), nor, particularly, is such a status remotely true for Hausa. Genetic classification is now known to be emphatically not impossible for "savage" languages (p. 155). Sturtevant would certainly have altered these lines;[13] after all, he witnessed and applauded the staking-out of North America as a whole by Sapir, of Algonquian by Bloomfield, of Malayo-Polynesian by Dempwolff, of Athabaskan and Eyak by Hoijer and Li, of Zapotecan by Swadesh, of Gulf by Haas, and of Tanoan by Trager, not to mention further work by students of these and others.

It is the final chapter, on the trend of linguistic development, that is perhaps the most uneven for us today. The notion of progress in language (pp. 161 ff.) was very much in the air at that time but seems quite dated to us now (esp. p. 176). And yet the refusal to equate language with logic (p. 165) strikes a very modern chord. The critique of Mill (pp. 165–66) is especially revealing and instructive in showing a change in values and ideas. While we feel ourselves half-agreeing with Sturtevant in his reaction to Mill, we must part company with him on his enthusiasm for the unique superiority of the modern European languages. It is essential here to recall that, after centuries of holding unquestioned pride of place, at the turn of this century the classical languages had been forced to yield equality of privilege in the academic pecking-order to the modern literary languages. We thus see Sturtevant, the classicist, reacting with liberal enthusiasm and magnanimity—surely pardonable, if flaw it be!

We see, then, in the author of this book a scholar steeped in Latin and Greek, in the philological study of Old English, and in the Indo-European background of these languages as

13 Cf. his brief statement, *Introduction*, p. 164, § 236.

disclosed by a full century of linguistic science. And we see him standing on the threshold of an era which we now regard as the natural order and which he himself helped to shape, expounding the most exciting topic that the field of linguistics then knew—how languages change. But this book is not a museum piece.[14] The subject of linguistic change, while no longer the single paramount object of linguistic study, is still one of the basic fascinations that the field offers. Sturtevant's concise account of it wears well and is couched, moreover, in a wealth of examples drawn with urbanity from firsthand knowledge in depth of classical languages and cultures that may well arouse in younger readers a degree of surprise and wonder—perhaps even emulation!

ERIC P. HAMP

February, 1962

---

[14] Indeed, we cannot escape the somber thought that our schools and newspapers still behave largely as if men like Sturtevant had not yet lived and written.

PREFACE

This little book, which has grown out of lectures to students beginning their scientific study of language, is primarily intended as a textbook for similar introductory courses. It is hoped, however, that it will appeal to a wider public, and consequently technical terms and symbols that are not familiar to all educated people have been eliminated as far as possible. Some readers will be offended at the lack of any exact system of phonetic notation; but such a notation would have required a long explanation, which some readers would have skipped, and which would have caused others to lay the book aside. No real ambiguity seems to result from our attempt to use ordinary symbols and terms in their familiar values.

Since the book is the result of reading and thought extending over more than fifteen years, the author cannot now recall the source of each idea expressed. He is under obligation at some point or many to most of the standard works on linguistics. In addition to books mentioned in the text and to the handbooks which stand at the elbow of every linguist, we may specify Paul Passy's *Petite phonétique comparée* and Leonard Bloomfield's *An Introduction to the Study of Language.* Much of the book, perhaps more than the author is aware, is traceable to the classroom lectures of Professors William Gardner Hale, Frank Frost Abbott, and Carl Darling Buck. Dr. W. M. Patterson has read and

corrected the section on rhythm.   Professors Roland G.
Kent and Charles Knapp have read the book in manu-
script, and their criticism has improved it in many
places.   Professor Knapp has also read the proof.

E. H. STURTEVANT

COLUMBIA UNIVERSITY
July, 1917

ANALYTICAL TABLE OF CONTENTS

CHAPTER I

INTRODUCTION ON THE NATURE OF LANGUAGE

Relation between Speech and Writing

There is a widespread impression that the written word is the norm or model of human speech while the spoken word is a more or less faulty imitation. It is not hard to see how such a feeling originated. Written discourse, particularly if printed, is in general composed by the more gifted and careful members of a community, and people take more pains with their style in writing than in speaking. Then again, the content of books is as a rule more interesting and valuable than that of ordinary speech. In the experience of most of us conversation is trivial and ungrammatical, while written language has some value and is usually correct. So the feeling has spread abroad that the language of books is the norm on which speech should be modeled and by which it must be judged, and to a certain extent this feeling is justified.

As a matter of fact, however, whether we think of the history of human speech in general or of the linguistic experience of the individual speaker, spoken language is the primary phenomenon, and writing is only a more or less imperfect reflection of it. We all learn to understand speech before we learn to read, and to speak before we learn to write. We all hear more language than we read and speak a great deal more than we write. Spoken language is ordinarily more flexible than written language; it leads the way in linguistic development, while written language follows at a greater or less interval. The exact relationship between the two will be clearer if we examine briefly the origin and development of writing.

Development of Alphabets

The picture-language of the American Indians belongs to the most primitive type, in which the sense is entirely independent of spoken language—in order to

FIG. 1

understand a document it is not necessary to know the language of the writer, but merely to be familiar with the general principles of the system. Fig. 1 is a reproduction of a letter from an Indian chief to the president of the United States,[1] the original of which is in colors. Figures are inserted for convenience of reference. The identity of the recipient of the letter (8) is indicated by the fact that he has a white face and stands in

[1] Reproduction and interpretation (in the main) are from School-craft, *Historical and Statistical Information Respecting the Indian Tribes of the United States*, I, 418 ff.; cf. Wundt, *Völkerpsychologie, Die Sprache*[2], I, 235 f.

a white house, that is, "to the white man in the White House." The writer (1) identifies himself as belonging to a tribe of the eagle totem and marks himself as a chief by the lines rising from his head; his extended arm denotes an offer of peace and friendship. The four eagles behind (2, 3, 4, 5) represent warriors of his, who are also of the eagle totem. The figure in the rear (6) represents another warrior, who is of the catfish totem. No. 9 is pictured merely as a man instead of being identified by his totem. That he, as well as No. 1, is a chief is shown by the lines rising from his head, and their number indicates that he is the more powerful of the two. The lines connecting the eyes of the various persons indicate harmony of view and purpose. The houses under three of the warriors indicate that they will hereafter live in houses, that is, will become civilized. The letter may be read as follows: "I, a chief of the eagle totem, several of my warriors, who belong to the eagle totem, another of the catfish totem, and a certain chief who is more powerful than I, are assembled and offer our friendship to you, the white man in the White House. We all hold the same views and hope that you will too. Three of my warriors intend to live in houses." Several of these ideas are more explicitly put in our verbal interpretation than in the original pictograph, but there is no doubt as to the general purport of the letter.

The development of alphabetic signs from such a system as this can be most easily seen in Egyptian. We cannot actually trace the evolution in the extant texts; for the Egyptian system of writing changes only in unessential details in the more than four thousand years that are covered by our records. But the system in use from the earliest monuments down contains clear traces of its origin and prehistoric development.

It is only rarely that one meets in Egyptian anything really analogous to the Indian picture-writing, but there are enough such cases to show that Egyptian has passed through a similar stage. For example, the sign for the west ⚑ has arms attached with which it is offering bread 𓏠. That is similar to the device which we have just seen in the Indian chief's letter, and its significance is equally independent of any particular language. If modern scholars are able to attach some phonetic value to such a sign, that is merely because they have learned elsewhere the Egyptian words involved.

Ordinarily an Egyptian symbol does not, as in this case, express a sentence, but at most a single word; and there are symbols for verbs and pronouns as well as for nouns. Many of the word-signs are pictures, pure and simple, and consequently are independent of speech. Thus ⚭ means "eye" or "oculus" or "Auge" as much as it does Egyptian "ʾirt." Other purely pictorial symbols are ⊙ "sun," 𓄤 "front," ♀ "face," ⌒ "mouth."

The first essential connection with spoken language is to be recognized in the use of a pictorial word-sign for a second word of similar sound. The sign ⌑ is the ground plan of a house and represents the idea "house" directly. It was, however, closely associated with the word *pr*[1]

---

[1] The Egyptian phonetic signs never indicate the vowels, and so we are almost entirely ignorant as to the number and character of the vowels in the various words whose consonantal skeletons have been recorded. One must supply enough vowels to make the words pronounceable, and it is customary to employ the vowel *e* for this purpose.

"house," and came to be employed for the phonetically similar verb *prj* "to go out."

A further step is seen in the use of pictorial word-signs in a phonetic value to denote parts of longer words. The sign ⊏⊐ means *mn* "draughtboard," but it is regularly used for the combination *mn* in any word that is written phonetically. Similarly ⊓ denotes the sound-group *pr* as well as the words *pr* "house" and *prj* "to go out;" ⊛ denotes the sound-group *hr* as well as the word *hr* "face."

The "alphabetic" symbols for the single consonants originated in the same way. The sign ⊏⊐ means primarily *š*ᵓ¹ "lake, tank," but it is also used for the sound *š* in any word. ⊂⊃ means *r*ᵓ "mouth" and also, with neglect of the weaker consonant, the sound *r*. The Egyptians had alphabetic symbols for all their consonants, and it would have been easy to write the language with these alone. The priestly scribes, however, always combined the other methods of writing with this one, chiefly, no doubt, because they did not realize the advantages of phonetic writing, but partly also because the picture symbols were both decorative and mysterious.

Whether the Egyptian hieroglyphs ever actually gave rise to a real alphabetic system in the hands of Semitic or Cretan borrowers we do not know. But it is probable that the Phoenician alphabet, whether it was borrowed from Egypt or not, and also every other

---

¹ The sound *š* was similar to English *sh*. By ᵓ we mean to indicate the glottal stop which is represented by Hebrew aleph and which is heard in German as the initial of words which in writing begin with a vowel. The sound is produced by impounding the breath behind the vocal chords and suddenly releasing it.

system of phonetic writing has passed through a development similar to that which we can reconstruct for the Egyptian of more than six thousand years ago.

Even if the Egyptians had thrown away all of their hieroglyphs except the signs for the consonants, their system of writing would still have been very imperfect in that it would not have indicated the vowels. Such purely consonantal writing is actually seen in the Phoenician and Hebrew alphabet; for the use of vowel-points in writing Hebrew is a modern refinement.

If, according to tradition, the Greeks borrowed their alphabet from the Phoenicians, they made good the lack of vowel-signs. And yet the Greek alphabet was far from perfect. In its earliest stages it did not denote vowel quantity at all, and even in its developed form a majority of the vowels were not marked as long or short. Accent was not indicated until Alexandrian times and then very imperfectly. There was never any attempt to indicate syllable division. We are certain of several further serious lacks, and, if our knowledge of Greek pronunciation were more extensive, we could no doubt detect still others.

Imperfections of Alphabets

That the English alphabet is very imperfect everyone knows, but how great its shortcomings are is not so obvious. Although we are in the habit of thinking that such a word as "ran" has only three sounds corresponding to its three letters, phonographic and other records of speech-sounds show, in the first place, that there is no division of a word into parts and, in the second place, that the pronunciation constantly changes throughout the word. No two vibrations of the initial *r*-sound are precisely alike, although the *r*-vibrations are far more nearly like one another than like the *a*-vibrations. Between the two groups of vibrations there is an intermediate territory which resembles both *r* and *a* in some degree. We can convince ourselves of the truth of these observations by pronouncing the word "ran" very slowly and noticing the gradual alteration of sound from *r* to *a*. We cannot fix any boundary between the two, and we cannot pick out any moment as representing a pure *a* unmixed with either *r* or *n*. In order to represent speech perfectly an alphabet would have to indicate several varieties of *r* and of *a* and also the intermediate stages between them. It would have to contain so many symbols that its use for practical purposes would be very difficult indeed.

No known alphabet represents speech-sounds even as accurately as would be convenient. They all exhibit such imperfections as the representation of a single sound by several signs (English "zinc," "as"), the representation of several sounds by a single sign (English "cart," "city"), the representation of a simple sound by a combination of signs (English *th*), or the representation of a combination of sounds by a single sign (English *x*). There are five chief causes of the imperfection of alphabets:

1. As alphabets are an outgrowth of picture-writing they are almost certain to have in their earlier stages several signs for the same sound. For example, Egyptian has at least four ways of representing the sound-group *nw;* either Ƽ or ⌒ has this value. The alphabetic signs ⅋ are theoretically possible, but

scarcely occur together without additional characters. Either of the following combinations, however, may be employed: ⊙⟩, ⌒⊙⟩ .

2. Alphabets grow up at a time when there is no scientific system of phonetics—no clear idea of how many and what sounds require representation. When certain signs began to be used for vowels in early Greece, no account was taken of the important difference between long and short vowels. Either men were not fully conscious of the difference, or it did not seem to them of sufficient importance to require representation.

3. All known alphabets have been borrowed from some foreign source, and, since no two languages employ precisely the same sounds, an alphabet which suits one language tolerably well is inadequate for another. Sometimes the borrowing people fill in the gaps by newly invented signs. This seems to have been the case with Greek φ for *ph* (pronounced nearly as in "haphazard") and with Anglo-Saxon þ and ð for *th* (pronounced as in "thin" or as in "thine"). Sometimes a combination of several signs is used to represent the peculiar sounds of the borrowing language. In the early Greek inscriptions of Thera the aspirate which was elsewhere and later represented by φ is written by a group of two signs ΠΗ. Again, the difficulty is sometimes avoided by the use of a sign in several values with or without diacritical marks to differentiate them. The Oscans borrowed their alphabet from their Etruscan neighbors, who had no vowel *o* and consequently no sign for that sound. The Oscans made good the lack by employing

the sign V for *o* as well as for *u;* after a while the letter
came to be written V in case it stood for *o.*

4. When a system of writing has once become
familiar, there is a tendency to stick to it, even if the
pronunciation changes. Examples of this may be seen
in almost any written language. In Latin the diphthong *ei* became long *i* about 150 B.C., but the spelling
with *ei* was in common use till the beginning of the
Christian era. We see this natural conservatism pushed
to a ridiculous extreme in the traditional spelling of
French and English. In English we not only continue
to write numerous letters that have not represented any
actual sound for hundreds of years, but we have besides
introduced silent letters into certain words which never
had the corresponding sounds. The word "doubt" is a
French loan-word, and therefore the most archaic
spelling we could expect in English is that of the French
doute, but a *b* has been introduced by some schoolmaster
who wanted to exhibit his knowledge of Latin *dubito.*

5. Sometimes foreign words are retained in writing
after they come to be translated in speech. We write
"etc." for *et cetera,* "e.g." for *exempli gratia,* "i.e." for
id est, but we read "and so forth," "for example," "that
is." In Persia in the time of the Sassanians the written
language consisted largely of Aramaic words, although
the spoken language was Persian.

In consequence of the first three factors just discussed
all known systems of alphabetic writing have been more
or less imperfect at the outset, and in consequence of
the last two factors (especially the fourth) they constantly tend to become less and less faithful representa-
tives of speech. If there were no contrary tendency,

alphabetic writing would ultimately become as arbitrary and difficult as the systems out of which it developed. This unfortunate result is obviated only by a series of more or less thorough spelling reforms, each of which is succeeded by a longer or shorter period during which the written language again remains nearly stationary, and the spoken language continues its development. Consequently it is only the spoken language that has any independent existence, while nearly all systems of writing are the result of a compromise between tradition and the phonetic representation of speech. Linguistic science is therefore primarily concerned with spoken language. Written language is important for our purpose only in so far as by its help we can restore the spoken language of which it is an imperfect representation. But, since linguistic science deals very largely with linguistic change, it is necessary to compare different stages in the development of the several languages; and these are preserved only in writing except for the phonographic records that have been made since the invention of the phonograph in the year 1877. It is therefore an essential part of the task of the science to establish the phonetic value of the symbols by which the languages of the past are recorded. This has been done with considerable accuracy for many languages, although in every case numerous details are still undetermined.

The Analysis of Language

If asked to describe the structure of language, many would say that the simplest linguistic unit is a letter or the sound represented by a letter and that one or more sounds make a syllable, one or more syllables make a word, one or more words make a sentence, one or more sentences make a paragraph, etc. This way of looking at the matter was nearly universal until a few decades ago, but is really no more accurate than to describe the structure of man by saying that the simplest human element is a cell, that several cells make an organ or limb, and that several organs and limbs make a man. In nature one finds only whole men and can observe their various parts only by means of anatomy or by a sort of mental analysis. Just so we talk only in sentences, and the smaller divisions of language have no independent existence.

All long sentences, however, are broken by pauses into several phrases which correspond with logical divisions of the thought. Of the linguistic units smaller than a phrase, the only one which is perceptibly marked off in speech is the syllable. We are not yet ready to define the syllable or to discuss the means by which syllables are marked off from one another; but that they are marked off is perfectly obvious to all. Metrical form and rhythm in speech or song depend upon syllabification; in fact, many kinds of verse involve an actual counting of syllables.

A word, on the other hand, is not marked off from the rest of the phrase. There is scarcely any difference in our usual pronunciation between the phrases "an iceman" and "a nice man," "I scream" and "ice cream," between the phrase "at all" and the first two syllables of the phrase "a tall man" (for example, "he's not a tall man," "he's not at all bad"). The word "apron" is derived from French *naperon;* for "a napron" was misunderstood "an apron." Similarly "auger"

comes from Anglo-Saxon *nafu-gar*, and "adder" is the
same word as German *Natter*. By the reverse process
"an ekename" has become "a nickname," and "an
ewt" has become "a newt." The phrase "that other"
has given rise to the colloquial "the tother." One
result of the fact that words are not marked off from
one another in pronunciation is that verse and music
are ordinarily indifferent to word divisions provided that
the syllables and accents are right.

In one respect, however, words have a more independent existence than the parts of a man or an animal.
Whereas a live nose or finger or foot can have no existence
except as parts of a larger whole, it is quite possible for a
word to stand alone, that is, to constitute an entire
sentence. Among the sentences first learned in child-
hood are such as these: "mama!" "come!" "go!"
"drink!" "naughty!" It is no wonder, then, that when
a child hears such sentences as "mama comes," "mama
goes," "drink milk," "drink water," he soon learns to
recognize the already familiar sound-complexes in their
new surroundings. Thus, too, he soon learns to analyze
new combinations of old material for himself; a little
boy with no sisters knows well the sentences "naughty
boy," "naughty baby," "naughty hand," and he will
at once understand the sentence "naughty girl."
Soon, indeed, he will make new combinations of his
own, such as "naughty spoon," "naughty milk,"
"naughty mama." At a somewhat later stage of
development a child will promptly isolate the unfamiliar
element in a sentence. He has heard "see the dog!"
"see the baby!" "see the boy!" and when he hears for
the first time "see the moon!" he follows the direction

to look for something and tries to find out the meaning of the word "moon."

Why is it that words can be so readily separated from one another if they are not separated in pronunciation? One reason is that each word, while keeping its own form intact, appears in constantly varying surroundings; a word is capable of being isolated from the rest of the sentence in much the same way as a tree or a rock can be distinguished from the rest of the landscape when the observer moves. A second reason why we recognize words as separate entities is that the thought expressed by the sentence varies with the form. The sentences "mother comes" and "mother goes" stand in the same relation to each other as the corresponding concepts; the two sentences contain a common word, and the two concept-groups contain a common concept. It is this fact which fixes the attention upon sentence analysis and leads young children to their really astonishing facility in so abstruse a logical process.

The importance of attention in the process of isolating words appears from the fact that the most common words of all, such as "is," "are," "in," "with," whose meaning is not very interesting in itself, are not among the first to be isolated. They probably stand in this respect about on a plane with the commoner prefixes and suffixes. For these are isolated in the same way as words. When a child has identified the words "boy" and "boy's," "girl" and "girl's," "baby" and "baby's," etc., he finally succeeds in isolating the genitive ending, that is, he associates the final s directly with the concept "belongs to."

There remain those linguistic elements which the ordinary observer regards as the simplest of all, that is,

the sounds of which a syllable is composed. These
sounds are not marked off from one another in pronunciation, and they have no such association with meaning
as would lead to their isolation during the process of
learning to speak.   The reason why those who know how
to read have some knowledge of speech-sounds is that,
to some extent, the letters of the alphabet represent
sounds.   But since the representation is very imperfect,
most readers and writers have but a vague and faulty
notion of phonetics.   We must not be so easily
contented.

Phonetics

Speech is produced by the expulsion of the breath
through the passages of the throat, mouth, and nose,
while these are modified in various ways.   The modification begins in the vocal chords of the larynx, the box at
the top of the windpipe which is popularly called the
"Adam's apple."   The vocal chords are two membranes
attached to the walls of the larynx in such a way that
they may be drawn together until they completely stop
the passage of the breath.   When the vocal chords are
so placed as to leave a narrow opening between them,
the breath sets them in rapid vibration and produces the
musical tone which we call voice.   One may convince
one's self that voice really originates in the Adam's
apple by placing a finger at that point and producing
the sound a; a slight vibration can be plainly felt.   If
the breath is expelled with some force while the vocal
chords are relatively near the position of rest, friction
produces the noise which we call a whisper.   When the
whisper is not modified by a narrowing of the mouth
passage, the result is aspiration, the sound of the letter h.

The voice produced by the vibration of the vocal chords is an element of all vowels, except whispered vowels, and of many consonants. The presence or absence of voice is often the sole or the chief distinction between two consonants; for example, between *z* and *s*, *v* and *f*, *b* and *p*, *d* and *t*. Speech-sounds may all be classed either as **voiced** or as **voiceless**.

After passing the vocal chords, the breath may pass through the nose or through the mouth or through both at once. All sounds produced with the nasal passage open are said to be **nasal**. The nasal vowels of French and of some other languages are produced with both the passages open. The nasal consonants are produced with the nasal passage open and the mouth passage closed; the difference between the consonants depends upon the place of closure.

All other speech-sounds are produced with the nasal passage closed and with more or less closure of the mouth. Certain sounds are produced by closing both passages completely and then opening the mouth with an explosion. To say *p* we first close the lips firmly and then suddenly open them and release the breath which had been imprisoned behind them. If the closure is made with the tongue against the gum at the roots of the upper teeth, the sound produced is *t*. If the closure is between the surface of the tongue and the roof of the mouth, the resulting sound is *k*. Such sounds are called indifferently **explosives**, **stops**, or **mutes**. Some of them are voiceless (*p*, *t*, *k*), while others are voiced (*b*, *d*, *g*).

In the production of many sounds the closure is incomplete, so that the breath is not entirely stopped, but merely makes a rubbing sound as it passes through the narrowed part of the mouth passage. If one makes an incomplete closure with the tongue against the tip of the upper teeth, the sound produced is *th* without voice, as in "thin," or with voice, as in "this." Such sounds are called **spirants**.

The closure or partial closure of the mouth passage may be made at many different points. (1) With the lips together we produce **labials** (*p, b, wh, w*). (2) With the lower lip against the upper teeth we produce **labio-dentals** (*f, v*). (3) **Dentals** are formed with the tongue against the tips of the upper teeth (*th*). (4) With the tongue against the gum above the upper teeth **alveolars** are produced (*t, d*). (5) With the tip of the tongue turned back toward the hard front palate we pronounce **cacuminals** (American *r*). (6) **Palatals** are formed with the surface of the tongue near or against the hard palate (*y* in "yet"). (7) With the surface of the tongue against the soft palate we produce **velars** (*k, g*). In addition to these positions of closure, several others are employed in various foreign languages. Thus a contact farther back than the velar position gives (8) the **uvulars** of Arabic and other oriental languages. It is possible to pronounce many more than the English sounds with the contact-positions that are usual in English. German has a voiceless palatal spirant (*ch* in *ich*) and a voiceless velar spirant (*ch* in *ach*). The Hindoo languages have cacuminal stops (*t, d*). French and German have an alveolar *r*. In French and German *t* and *d* are dentals instead of alveolars.

There are in several cases different ways of making a partial closure in about the same place. Both *s* and *l* are alveolars; the difference between them is that, while for *s* the closure is complete at the sides of the mouth, for *l* the closure is complete in front and incomplete at the sides; *l* is therefore called a **lateral**.

In our table of English consonants, we omit *h*, which involves no closure of the mouth passage, and the compound sounds *ch*, as in "church" ($=t+sh$) and *j*, as in "judge" ($=d+zh$).

TABLE OF ENGLISH CONSONANTS

	Labial	Labio-Dental	Dental	Alveolar	Cacuminal	Palatal	Velar
Nasals........	*m*	......	......	*n*	......	*n* in "pinion"	*ng*
Stops:							
Voiceless....	*p*	......	......	*t*	......	......	*k*
Voiced......	*b*	......	......	*d*	......	......	*g*
Spirants:							
Voiceless....	*wh*	*f*	*th*	*s, sh, l*	*r*	*y*	......
Voiced......	*w*	*v*	*th*	*z, zh, l*	*r*	*y*	......

While some consonants are spoken with and others without voice, all English **vowels** are normally voiced. Another striking difference between the two classes of sounds is that the vowels are spoken with the mouth passage wider open than it ever is in producing consonants.

In this respect, however, there is much difference between the vowels themselves, and they are therefore arranged according to their degree of **openness**. The closest vowels are *u*, which is but slightly more open than *w*, and *i*, which is barely distinguished from *y*. The most open sound of all is that of *a* in "father." The other vowels hold intermediate positions.

The difference between *i* and *u* is in the place of closure. The former is produced by bringing the surface of the tongue almost as near to the hard palate as in pronouncing *v*, and *u* is formed with the lips almost as near together as in *w*. We do not, however, call *u* a labial vowel; in the production of both *w* and *u* there is an approximation of the back of the tongue to the soft palate, and in the case of the vowel this narrowing of the vocal passage is more important than the other (it is possible to pronounce a recognizable *u* with the lips wide apart). On account of this latter closure *u* is called a **back vowel**, while *i* is a **front vowel**. All other vowels stand between the two extremes.

On the basis of these two criteria we may arrange most of the English vowels as follows:

	Front		Back
Close (machine)	i		u (r*u*le)
	(p*i*n) i		u (f*u*ll)
	(p*a*y) ay		ow (thr*ow*)
	(m*e*n) e		o (*o*bey)
	(c*a*t) a	aw (l*aw*)	
Open		(*a*sk) a	a(f*a*ther)

Two of the foregoing sounds are really diphthongs, although most speakers of English are unaware of that fact. If the reader will pronounce long *o* slowly while looking into a mirror or while touching his lips with his finger, he will find that his lips gradually approach each other until they are in the position for pronouncing *w*. The conventional spelling of "throw" is therefore phonetically correct, while that of "old" is misleading. Similarly we have a diphthong in "pay," in spite of our usual preference for the spelling seen in "page." It is necessary to include these diphthongs in our table, since English does not possess the simple sounds of German and French long *o* and long *e*. The vowel of "law," on the other hand, is not a diphthong, but is written with two characters in our table merely for clearness. We have not included those diphthongs whose prior elements appear also by themselves, *ai* (in "right"), *awi* (in "oil"), *au* (in "cow").[1]

The foregoing classification is based solely upon the position of the organs in producing the several sounds. It is also possible to classify the vowels according to their acoustic properties. The timbre or characteristic quality of the several vowels is independent of the musical tone produced by the vocal chords, and it depends chiefly upon two groups of factors. Each vowel gets secondary tone or overtone from the resonance chamber of the mouth, and this overtone is constant for a given vowel in the pronunciation of a given speaker, and the intervals between the overtones of the several vowels are the same for all speakers of a given dialect. It is easy to observe the overtones of the vowels if one whispers them, since then there is no musical tone coming from the vocal chords. If, now, one whispers the vowels in our table, one after another, beginning at the left, it will be observed that their pitch constantly falls.

With the overtones of the vowels are combined certain other noises, which we need not now consider.

It is possible to produce vowels with the mouth in other positions than those we have been considering. For example, a vowel may be a close vowel but formed

---

[1] The final elements in these diphthongs are really more open than ordinary *i* and *u;* they might equally well be written *e* and *o*.

midway between front and back; in fact, there may be a whole series of sounds between *i* and *u*, between the initial sounds of the diphthongs *ay* and *ow*, and between *e* ("men") and *o* ("obey"). Such vowels are German *ü*, French *u* (between *i* and *u*) and German *ö*, French *eu* (between *o* and *e*). They are called **abnormal** vowels. The vowel of English "club" and "summer" is an abnormal vowel not very different from the *a* of "father," but closer.

The familiar classification of vowels as long or short is quite distinct from the matters which we have been discussing. A long vowel is simply one which is held for a relatively long time. There may therefore be an indefinite number of degrees of length. The traditional division of vowels into two quantitative classes probably never fitted any language; that it did not fit Latin and Greek is shown by the numerous forms of verse which permit spondees (--) in the same line with iambs (ᵕ-) or trochees (-ᵕ). In English we may observe three degrees of quantity in "not," "naught," and "gnawed."

A difference in quantity appears, not only in vowels, but also in all consonants except the stops. Long consonants are not common in English, except in compounds such as "illegal," "unknown," "unnatural," and in such phrases as "some more," "our rights." The common description of such sounds as double consonants has some justification in the fact that the syllable division falls within them and makes them appear to be divided into two parts.

Some scholars speak also of long stops, but here the splitting of the sound into two parts is so striking that the common name of double sounds is better. A stop is produced by two acts: the closing of the mouth passage and the sudden opening of it. Neither of these acts can be prolonged; but, when the stop is doubled, there is a slight pause between the closure and the opening during which no sound is produced. Double stops occur in English under the same circumstances as long consonants, for example, "rat-trap," "a good deed."

The various speech-sounds differ from one another in **sonorousness,** that is, in the amount of sound. It is easier to hear the vowels than the consonants, and consequently children who are just learning to speak pronounce their vowels better than their consonants. For the same reason it is of the utmost importance for a public speaker to pronounce his vowels distinctly; he can make his hearers understand them under circumstances which make the hearing of some consonants impossible, and the hearers will then be able to supply such of the consonants as they have not been able to hear. The voiced consonants are more easily heard than the unvoiced, the open vowels than the close. The least sonorous sound is *h*. These variations are to be observed in case the energy of pronunciation remains constant.

But it is possible, of course, to speak a given sound so that it will be heard more easily or less so, by simply increasing or diminishing the force of the breath, that is, the **stress** of pronunciation. The resultant of these two factors is the **intensity** of speech. During a sentence the intensity constantly varies in a series of waves of uneven height. These waves are the **syllables.** In

other words, the syllable divisions are points of less
intensity than the neighboring sounds. If the syllable
division falls within a long consonant ("illegal," "unnatural"), that is due solely to a lessening of stress. In
most cases, however, there is a decrease of sonorousness
at the syllable division. Note the difference between
"un-til," "ant-hill," and "in-stil." If a consonant of
greater sonorousness stands between two consonants of
less sonorousness, the group constitutes a syllable, as in
"likened," in which the second syllable contains no vowel.
A consonant is the most sonorous sound also in the
second syllable of "letter," "little," "heaven," and many
other words.

The last-mentioned word, however, may be pronounced as one syllable by reducing the stress of *n* until
its intensity falls below that of *v*. It is more difficult to
reduce "letter" to one syllable, because of the greater
difference in sonorousness between *t* and *r*, and such a
pronunciation is never heard in English.

While each syllable wave involves an increase of
intensity, the maximum of intensity, that is, the height
of the wave, varies from syllable to syllable. Here, as
elsewhere, intensity depends partly upon sonorousness
and partly upon stress. A familiar term for stress as it
applies to syllables is **accent**.

The latter word was originally used of a very different
modification of syllables; for Latin *accentus* is derived
from *cano* "sing," and was used to translate Greek
προσῳδία "pitch." The word is still used in this sense,
especially in the phrase, **pitch accent**. An increase
in stress is usually accompanied by a rise in pitch,
and in some languages, as Latin, the two variations

are so nearly equal in importance that they may be treated together under the term accent. In other languages, as in English, the rise in pitch is slight, and the increase in stress is relatively strong. In still other languages the variation in pitch is great, and the variation in stress is so slight as to have no importance. This was the case with ancient Greek.

The foregoing remarks, however, apply merely to syllabic accent. Even languages like English, which have scarcely any pitch accent, nevertheless make extensive use of variation in pitch for modifying the meaning of sentences and phrases, as in the "rising inflection" of certain kinds of questions.

Relation between Form and Meaning

One of the first linguistic problems to attract the attention of the thinkers of ancient Greece was this: Do the meanings of words belong to them inherently and naturally, or have men merely agreed to attach certain meanings to certain words? The question is discussed in Plato's *Cratylus*, but the controversy began before his time. It is not strange that men should have seen something inevitable in the meanings of words; for no man can change them. We may call a man a horse and a horse a man; but both we and all who hear us will be quite conscious that we are speaking incorrectly. Even if a community should pass a law that the word "horse" should hereafter mean "man," the law would be almost as absurd and quite as ineffectual as the bill once introduced in a certain legislature that the area of a circle should equal the square of one-fourth of its circumference.

Nevertheless it is perfectly certain that the meaning of words is not ordained by nature. To say nothing of homonyms, such as English "mine" and "sun" ("son"), or of the difference in meaning between Latin *tu* and English "two" and between Latin *laus* and English "louse," it cannot be true that a single object is naturally and inevitably named "sun" in English, *sol* in Latin, *Sonne* in German, *soleil* in French, etc. Somehow or other the meaning of each word is a matter of convention.

In some cases this is obvious enough. There is general agreement among scientists that the discoverer of a new species or a new element has the right to name it. In other matters different scholars are likely to invent rival terms for the same idea. In grammar there has gradually grown up a perfect forest of technical terms, so that, in the hope of making it once more possible to see through the undergrowth, a committee of grammarians has recently devised a uniform system of terminology. In some of the South Sea Islands it is forbidden to speak the name of the reigning monarch or any word that resembles his name. If then a new king's name resembles the word for "house" or "bread" or "father," a new word has to be agreed upon.

The reason why we do not more often witness these linguistic agreements is simply that most of them were made before we were born. Each generation adopts a few of its own, but in general it merely accepts the conventions of an earlier day.

Imitation

For the most part, then, each generation gets its language from the preceding generation by imitation, just as it learns all the other activities of life. For speech is from the start quite on a par with the rest of our customs; all are learned in the same way. At first a child's movements have little resemblance to those of his elders, and the sounds of his first meaningless prattle are very much more numerous and diverse than the sounds of any language. Little by little he acquires the bodily motions which he sees in others, and his sounds come more and more to resemble the speech-sounds which he hears. As he grows older, he imitates more closely the particular ways of eating, walking, and sitting that are employed by his elders; for example, it is as easy for a child to sit on the floor as in a chair, but, since grown people sit in chairs, he too wants a chair. At the same time the child learns to speak more and more precisely in the manner of the community.

Throughout life we are governed in all our actions by the customs of our associates. The influence of imitation in matters of dress has often been discussed, but few realize how far-reaching it is. Men sometimes blame women for following the rapidly shifting fashions of women's dress, and women sometimes ridicule men for adhering to the stupidly rigid custom of wearing coats in summer. The women usually retort that they like a little change and that there is really something to be said for the latest type of skirt or hat. Men say that they really do not mind a coat, even in hot weather. Both imply that they could defy the fashions if they chose; but, as a matter of fact, we cannot without great discomfort dress in any but the usual way. I once found it convenient to wear an academic cap for a trip of two miles along the streets and in public vehicles, but the experience was so uncomfortable that I borrowed a hat for my return trip.

Just as fashions in dress are binding upon all members of a given class and are imitated by all who look up to that class, so fashions in language are binding upon all people of culture and are followed by other members of the community to the best of their ability. This is irksome for those who rise from a lower to a higher class in the community, or who go from a provincial neighborhood to a college or university. It is not easy, and it often seems quite useless or even disloyal to one's origin, to alter one's speech at the behest of fashion; but in many cases the thing must be done. Actors with an American accent cannot easily secure an engagement in England. A strong western *r* is a distinct hindrance to a man who is trying to make his way in the East or the South of the United States, while a Bostonian pronunciation is not tolerated in some circles in Chicago.

It is sometimes supposed that the tyranny of fashion is of recent growth, or at least that it is confined to civilized society. Many have sighed for the freedom in matters of dress that is supposed to belong to savage life. It is true that sudden and violent changes of fashion are of recent date, but the decrees of fashion were formerly even more peremptory than they are today. It would, in fact, be difficult to find a period when there has been greater variety of dress among people of a given class than there is now, or when departures from the mode have been more leniently treated. Among savages a variation from the usual form of loin cloth or nose ring is almost unthinkable; for among them the individual is nothing, the tribe everything.

Fashion in speech follows similar laws. In a group of savages there is scarcely any individual variation, although there may be differences between the speech of men and of women, between that of the old and of the young. With us individual variations are rather the rule than the exception; almost any chance gathering of educated people includes persons of different linguistic training and habits. Many a variation from the norm, however, is felt to be almost serious enough to exclude a man from polite society; such, for example, are "ain't," "them people," "me and him was there." Many other variations are disapproved but tolerated, for example, the New Englander's "lawr" and "idear," the Westerner's "carrt," the Kentucky "kyaht," the Alabama "cawt." In many other cases we hear a pronunciation different from our own and can scarcely tell which of the two we prefer; is "int'resting" preferable to "interèsting?"

If the tyranny of fashion has relaxed its rigor, it has enormously extended the territory over which its decrees are binding. The modistes of Paris are supreme in Berlin, San Francisco, and Buenos Aires, and a linguistic fashion that is set in London is followed in New York and Cape Town. The civilized world of today is divided into relatively few communities, some of which are larger than any that have previously existed.

This development has been made possible by the increased intercourse between different parts of the world; there has been an enormous growth of commerce and travel, which has brought into intimate personal relationship great numbers of men who dwell far apart.

Even those who live all their lives in one locality come to know many persons from a distance and are thus subjected to the influence of the fashions of places which they have never seen. Furthermore, those members of the community who travel most are in general the very ones who are most respected and imitated. Consequently it is the most influential part of society which exerts its influence for uniformity.

Intercourse by the written word is also increasing with unexampled rapidity; all educated persons come almost daily into contact with language from distant regions, either in letters, newspapers, and magazines, or in pamphlets and books. This sort of intercourse, however, does not affect all linguistic phenomena, but only those which are reflected in writing, that is, word-meaning, vocabulary, and syntax. Pronunciation remains unaffected because it is not indicated; the native of New Orleans reads aloud a letter from Boston precisely as he would a letter from Baton Rouge. Correspondence and literature cannot make for uniformity of pronunciation until our orthography is phonetic and each writer conscientiously indicates his own pronunciation.

The influence of literature is re-enforced by the schools; for in general the teachers inculcate the usage of the best writers. Effective pedagogy, however, calls for a certain amount of dogmatism, and so the teachers often erect a literary tendency into a rule that must have no exceptions; hence such classroom bogeys as "it's me" or the "split infinitive."

Imitation is in general a conservative factor. It does, to be sure, frequently spread an innovation—a bronze shoe polish, a mincing gait, a morsel of slang, or a habit of making statements with a rising inflection. But as long as all members of the community confine themselves to imitating the fashions already set, no change can arise. Furthermore the conservative force of imitation varies in proportion to the size of the community; for each innovation is opposed by the influence of that part of the community which is as yet unaffected by it, and the larger the community the larger the majority against each incipient change.

Change in Language

We might suppose, then, that language would remain forever stationary. But everyone knows that languages change; the English of Shakespeare and of the King James version of the Bible is strikingly unlike the English of the present day, while Chaucer is scarcely intelligible without a glossary. It is our purpose to consider the causes and modes of linguistic change.

Since language is a purely conventional affair, maintained and handed down by imitation, changes in language must come from one of two sources. There may be a change in the model, that is, in the speech of the person or persons who at the moment set the linguistic fashion. Such innovations are constantly arising in the speech of each one of us. We call some of them mistakes; others, which are more intentional, we call forced uses of words or awkward sentences; still others, which are fully intentional, we call figures of speech or coined words or new phrases. Most of such innovations are purely momentary and have no influence upon the language, but every now and then one of them finds imitators. After a strenuous day of speechmaking in New Jersey, Mr. Roosevelt emphatically denied the suggestion that he was tired: "Why! I feel like a bull moose," he exclaimed. At the moment the phrase was effective, just because it was personal and original; there was no reason to suppose that it would gain more currency than any of the other similes for a tireless man. But the reporters adopted the phrase and turned it into a metaphor; they made Mr. Roosevelt himself a bull moose, and presently his followers were called by the same name. In all such cases there are two processes to be distinguished: the origin of the innovation in an individual speaker may be called a **primary change**; the spread of the innovation to other speakers may be called a **secondary change**.

The other possible source of linguistic change is a change of models; a new king may ascend the throne and his subjects begin to follow his speech rather than that of his predecessor; or a neighboring community may make such advances in power or in culture that people imitate its speech. A few generations ago the common model for American English was the pulpit, although the really great writers had better models and thus escaped the pomposity of their contemporaries. Nowadays we scarcely have a common model in America: some of us try to follow the usage of the great writers, others the usage of the English aristocracy, still others take Broadway or the sporting page of the newspapers for their model; but we are all agreed in avoiding the solemn style of our ancestors. Such a change as this has something foreign about it; an uninterrupted development of the pulpit style could scarcely have yielded present-day

American English in so short a time. Whether we be Anglo-maniacs or baseball fans, we have adopted an idiom that is in large part foreign to the speech of our ancestors. A change of models, then, involves a **mixture of dialects,** even if the new model is only slightly different from the old.

There is no question here of the origination of a change; the new model is in existence before it is chosen. The choice of the model is an important phenomenon which will claim our attention later on (pages 151 f.); but, as far as specific linguistic changes are concerned, dialect mixture involves only the spread by imitation which we have called secondary change.

Another division of the subject of linguistic change is based upon the speech-material affected. We have change in the form of words, change in the meaning of words, change in vocabulary, and change in syntax. Primary change and secondary change require separate treatment only as far as they apply to change in form. In all other cases secondary change is so simple that there is little to be said about it beyond what has already been said in the section on imitation (pages 24 ff.).

CHAPTER II

PRIMARY CHANGE OF FORM

Under this head we should treat only the momentary changes of form, most of which are unintentional and without permanent effect upon language. But we are confronted by a serious difficulty: there are no extensive collections of lapses available for any language except German. In 1895 Meringer and Mayer published under the title *Versprechen und Verlesen* lists of mistakes which they had observed, and in 1908 Meringer published supplementary lists under the title *Aus dem Leben der Sprache*. The data presented in these two books are of the utmost value, and those in the earlier one have been used by almost every writer on linguistic science in the last twenty years. No one, however, has hitherto published similar observations upon other languages, and Meringer himself notes that there is reason to believe that other languages follow different tendencies to some extent. Even for the German itself we may suspect that some curious gaps in Meringer's material are due in part to the personal equation. Some English examples have been collected by Bawden, "A Study of Lapses" in the *Psychological Review, Supplement* III, No. 4 (1900), but the rather scanty material is not presented in enough detail, and the classification is not satisfactory for linguistic purposes.

Fortunately the more permanent changes of linguistic form furnish an indirect record of many other mistakes in pronunciation; for we have seen that all of the former which are not due to dialect mixture originated in a momentary variation in the speech of an individual. We may therefore use as illustrations mistakes inferred from secondary linguistic change.

Mistakes during the Learning of a Language

Human hearing is barely adequate to the demands which language makes upon it. Although our public halls are built according to certain acoustic principles, many speakers have difficulty in making themselves heard by a large audience. Even if a speaker is fully understood, it does not follow that the audience hears all his speech-sounds; for we readily supply a great deal from our knowledge of the situation and of what the speaker is likely to say. It is for this reason that sometimes, when we seem to hear only fragments of a sentence and at first make so little out of it that we ask to have it repeated, the meaning nevertheless flashes upon us before the repetition comes. When we try to understand a list of unconnected words or an unfamiliar name, the difficulty of understanding is much increased; for in such cases we are dependent upon the sense of hearing alone: the mind can supply nothing.

A child is able to supply far less than an adult; at first he can add nothing at all to what his ears bring him, and it is only by degrees that he acquires familiarity with one sentence or phrase after another. In the meantime he is certain to misinterpret many of the sounds which come to his ears—to "hear" incorrectly. A certain child habitually said "I'n" for "I'm" until his seventh year. The pronunciation was not to be heard in his environment, and he showed no tendency to substitute *n* for *m* in other words; he must have understood "I'n" when those about him said "I'm." Another child of seven or eight who said "perpelicular" for "perpendicular" apparently reproduced what she thought she heard. Until my thirtieth year I pronounced "trough" as "trouth."[1] Until that time I had never realized that others said "trouf"; and even then I became aware of my mistake only by seeing a printed list of words with *gh* for the sound *f*. Such cases are probably rare among literate persons; I could not long have retained my illusion if it had not been for the curiously perverse spelling of the word "trough." With young children, however, such mistakes as "brof" for "broth" are very common, and many of them must last throughout life in the speech of illiterate persons.

When a child first undertakes to imitate speech-sounds, he doesn't know what muscles to use to secure the desired effect. He sees some few motions of the lips and the lower jaw, and that fact undoubtedly helps; for blind children are said to be slower than others in learning to talk. Still in the main a child can reproduce the sound he hears only by a process of trial and test. Small wonder that his first attempts are far from successful. If the child hears correctly the sound to be imitated he will not be permanently satisfied until he has himself produced what he conceives to be the same sound; but he may be content with an apparently or approximately identical sound produced by a faulty articulation. My daughter pronounced *th* with the

[1] Since writing this I have learned of another case of this mispronunciation.

tip of the tongue thrust forward between the teeth, and neither she nor any of the household became aware of the peculiarity until her twelfth year. Meringer reports several cases of children who pronounced *s* with the lips closed except for an opening at the right corner of the mouth. This articulation seems in the cases reported to have been acquired by imitation; but it probably started with some child's experiments in reproducing the sound.

The suffix seen in Latin *vehiclum* (the early form of *vehiculum*) was originally *-tlom*. Perhaps the change from *-tlom* to *-clom* was in the first place due to a defect of hearing. Possibly a child heard *-tlom* correctly and was satisfied with the approximation *-clom*, although we should not expect such satisfaction to be permanent. There is also a third possibility, which will serve to illustrate the complicated nature of many apparently simple linguistic phenomena. Perhaps the first attempt to reproduce the sound *-tlom* led to *-clom*, and then a correction was made by keeping the surface of the tongue in the *c*-position and at the same time putting the tip of the tongue in the *t*-position. The resulting sound would be much nearer the desired *-tlom* than the first attempt was, but the complicated articulation would be more liable to alteration than an ordinary *t*. A speaker who intended the combined articulation would frequently say *-clom* by mistake. Thus a faulty articulation of a nearly correct sound would form an intermediate step in the change. A similar case is dialectic German *dlauben* for *glauben;* it may have started with a child's defective hearing, possibly with a careless approximation to a sound correctly heard, or, more probably, with a defective articulation of a sound which was virtually the same as *gl*. Many cases of lisping probably began as a result of defective hearing, but in the later stages the lispers are likely to be conscious of their mistake, while not knowing how to correct it. Very few cases are due to physical defects.

The mispronunciations of an adult who learns a foreign language are similar in origin to the mistakes of children in learning their mother-tongue. It is said that in the minutes of several French societies the name of the poet Schiller occurs with an initial *G*, as if it began with a voiced sound (the *zh* of "azure"). Since French has a voiceless *sh*, one must assume that the secretaries of the several societies heard incorrectly.

No two languages employ precisely the same sounds, and therefore a foreigner knows no better than a child how to produce certain sounds in the language he is learning. But, instead of making a series of experiments, as a child would do, he usually substitutes the most similar sound in his own language. A Frenchman pronounces English "pin" so that it sounds to us more as if spelt "peen"; he is substituting the French close short *i* for the English open short *i*. The vulgar American "dis" and "dat" for "this" and "that" may have originated with foreigners who had no *th*-sound in their native languages.

Such phenomena as these really belong to the subject of dialect mixture; the man who learns a foreign language may be said to have adopted a new model, and the mixture results from the difficulty he has in giving up his earlier linguistic habits. But since his mistakes are inadvertent, they stand in the same relation to the language he is learning as do the mistakes of a child. As a rule the use of a language by foreigners who have imperfectly mastered it has little permanent influence upon that language; the foreign peculiarities are felt to be undesirable by all who hear them, and so they are rarely imitated except by way of caricature.

Associative Interference

While to the unscientific observer ideas appear to be simple bits of mental experience, they are really composite. The simplest psychological fact is a sensation, that is, a mental process which comes to consciousness by way of one of the organs of sense. Sensations do not occur singly; for example, if I touch a piece of ice, I get a sensation of cold and a sensation of pressure. If my eyes are open, I am at the same time getting some kind of a sight sensation. All these sensations combined form the basis of the perception "piece of ice." An idea is a remembered or imagined perception, and, as a perception is based upon sensations, so an idea is based upon remembered sensations. A given sensation occurs in a great many ideas. The sensation of cold forms part of the basis of the idea of "ice," of "snow," of "frost," of "winter," etc. When for any reason the brain cells concerned with the sensation of cold are excited, any one of the ideas based upon that sensation is likely to come into consciousness. Since the perception of "ice" involves such an excitation, that perception is likely to lead to the ideas "snow," "frost," "winter," etc. Ideas which tend to accompany or follow one another in consciousness are said to be associated, but the term **association of ideas** should not suggest to us that ideas are tied up in bundles as it were. Ideas are associated because they contain common elements.

It frequently happens that two associated ideas come into consciousness in such quick succession that the reactions of the second interrupt the still uncompleted reactions of the first. This process is known as associative interference.

Analogy

Oertel[1] tells of hearing Bishop Potter say "evoid" and at once correct himself, "both avoid and evade." The idea "evade" first entered consciousness and set up its reaction, the pronunciation of the word; then the idea "avoid" crowded out the first idea and interfered with its reaction. To state the same thing from the linguistic point of view, at first the word "evade" was the more prominent of the two in thought, and then "avoid" intruded its second syllable. Very often, as in this case, a sound which is common to both words acts as a sort of switch to facilitate the shift from one to the other. We may figure the process thus (after Oertel), using capital letters for the sounds actually spoken:

$$\begin{matrix} \text{E} \\ \text{a} \end{matrix} \bigvee \begin{matrix} \text{a de} \\ \text{OI D} \end{matrix}$$

Such a common element, however, is not necessarily present at the point where the shift occurs. Meringer and Mayer report *Abschnatt* resulting from the synonyms *Abschnitt* and *Absatz*.

A similar case which has become normal is English "female." In French, *mâle* and *femelle* have no ety-

[1] *Lectures on the Study of Language*, p. 167.

mological connection and only a slight similarity of form. When both words were borrowed by the English their close association in meaning changed *femelle* into "female." Viewed superficially the process may be described as a modification of the one word on the analogy of the other. The process is commonly called analogy or analogical change; and since this suggests correctly enough the linguistic result, it would scarcely be worth while to substitute a term more exactly descriptive of the psychological phenomena.

When two words interfere with each other in such a way that the resulting word contains about equal parts of both, the process is sometimes called **contamination.** Bawden (p. 23) reports the slips "liquals" from the contamination of "liquids" and "linguals," "ruvershoes" from "rubbers" and "overshoes," "dreeze" from "draft" and "breeze," "perple" from "persons" and "people," "spaddle" from "spank" and "paddle." "Beginning" and "commencement" yield "begincement." A negro politician combined "insinuation" and "innuendo" in "insinuendo."

Sometimes the result of associative interference between two words is identical in form with one of the words, and we detect the interference only by the combination of the meaning of one word with the form of the other. Thus "to rinse clothes" becomes "to wrench clothes," the two words being associated on the basis of the twisting motion which forms an element of both ideas. The boys whom Mark Twain has immortalized in *Tom Sawyer* say "marvels" for "marbles."

If the association which leads to analogical change involves a false theory of the etymology of the word affected, the change is said to be due to **popular ety-mology**. In Anglo-Saxon *guma* meant "man," and *brydguma* meant "bride-man"; but in the course of time *guma* fell out of use, and the second member of the compound was popularly connected with "groom"; hence modern "bridegroom." French *outrage* is connected with Latin *ultra*, being derived from **ultragium*[1] or **ultraticum* "excess." The English pronunciation with a full vowel in the unaccented syllable (contrast "usage," "courage") is due to a false etymology from "out" and "rage." Shakespeare's "mandragora" has become "mandrake" through a ridiculous connection with "man" and "drake." Latin *inuleus* "stag" became *hinuleus* through a popular etymology from *hinnus* "mule." Many people pronounce "carousal" as if it were "carry-Sal"; pronunciation, however, does not determine whether the synonymous "merry-go-round" is interpreted "Mary-go-round."

Many association groups are based, not upon meaning, but upon function, that is, upon what James[2] has termed the "transitive" parts of the stream of consciousness. Our thought moves now more, now less, rapidly, and the regions of less rapid change ("substantive" states of consciousness) stand out so much more vividly that we are in danger of thinking that they constitute the whole of the stream of consciousness. I awake and see the sunlight streaming in at the window. I wonder whether it is time to get up. I look at my watch. Here are three clearly marked states of con-

---

[1] An asterisk prefixed to a word indicates that the word does not occur; but is assumed to have existed.

[2] *The Principles of Psychology*, I, 243 ff.

sciousness, the perception of the sunlight, the thought of getting-up time, and the decision to look at the watch; but between these portions of the train of thought lie feelings of relation between "sunlight-streaming-through-the-window" and "is-it-time-to-get-up?"—between the latter and "look-at-my-watch."

The phrase "the road to Mandalay" represents or may represent three successive states of consciousness ("the road"—"direction"—"the goal") of which the first and third are substantive and the second transitive. In the phrase "John's book" the transitive state of consciousness is represented in connection with the first substantive state; the word "John's" has both word-meaning and the function of possession. Properly, the function of a word is the relation which it bears to its context. It is convenient, however, to extend the term to such semantic elements as number, person, and tense, which are really parts of the substantive states of con-sciousness (or of word-meaning), but which nevertheless determine to some extent the relationship of words to one another.

On the basis of meaning the word "feet" is associated with "foot" and more remotely with "hand" and the other words for parts of the body; but it is also associated on the basis of function with all other plurals. Just so all present participles form one association group and all genitives another. Such groups as these are impressed on the mind of all speakers from the very fact that they are expressed in language, and the strength of the association varies directly with the clearness of the lin-guistic expression. The speakers of the Latin language had a clearly defined association group composed of accusatives; every speaker associated *bovem* with *bonum*, *exercitum*, *hanc*, etc., just because most accusatives were marked by form, and the category had to be reckoned with almost every time a sentence was formed or heard. Consequently mistakes in the use of these forms were comparatively rare. In English, on the other hand, most accusatives are not distinguished by form, and therefore we have great difficulty in keeping "me," "us," "him," "her," "them," and "whom" in their proper place.

An analogical change of form resulting from a functional group is the childish "feets" for "feet." The familiar word "feet" is interfered with and altered by the associated words "hands," "lips," "books," "plates," etc. "Worser" and "lesser" are the irregular comparatives of "worse" and "less" modified by the influence of the regular type; by a strange chance "lesser" has become correct, that is, usual, while "worser" remains an outcast. Latin *fio* is conjugated in the present-stem tenses like an active verb; its meaning, however, is passive, and the present infinitive *fiere*, which was still used by Ennius, was remodeled into *fieri* under the influence of *amari*, *audiri*, etc.

In many cases the analogical influence of the functional group is a more complicated matter which we call **analogical creation**. A child in counting the various parts of his body says, "One hand, two hands; one ear, two ears; one lip, two lips; one foot, two *foots*." In this case we have, not a modification of something old, as in the case of "feets," but a new creation on the basis of a known relationship. The process may be stated as a problem in proportion:

"lip":"lips"="foot":x. The child gives the correct solution, "foots."

Such creations are very common in the speech of children and illiterate adults. Everyone has heard "catched" for "caught," "growed" for "grew," "oxes" for "oxen," "yous" for "you" plural, "littler," etc. "Brung" for "brought" arose from the proportion "sing":"sung"="bring":x. Latin *ipse* is a compound of *is* and a particle *pse*, and was originally declined *is-pse*, *ea-pse*, accusative *eum-pse*, *eam-pse*, etc. The nominative masculine became *ipse* by a process which we shall consider later, and then the other forms (except the neuter *ipsum*) were created on the analogy of *iste* and *ille*, that is, *iste*:*ista*=*ipse*:x.

It is often doubtful whether a change is due to the simpler or to the more complex sort of analogy—to mere associative interference or to analogical creation. The occasional pronunciation "naytional" is of course due to the word "nation"; but it may be either a modification of "nătional" with associative interference by "nation," or it may be a new derivative from "nation" on the model of such pairs as "convention":"conventional," "culture":"cultural." There is similar doubt about the origin of "preférable" with the accent of "prefer," and of Latin *consacro* with the vowel of *sacro*, in place of the regular form *consecro*. The original genitive of the Latin fourth declension was the form in -*ūs*. In Plautus we find also the endings -*ī* and -*uis* which come, respectively, from the second declension and the third. These forms may be analogical creations: *amicus*:*amici*=*fructus*:x (*fructi*), *seni* (dative):*senis*=*anui* (dative):x (*anuis*). But it is also possible that the old genitives *fructus* and *anus* were present to consciousness when the new forms were first pronounced and were altered by the simultaneous remembrance of a word or words with the same function. In many instances, no doubt, both processes co-operate in originating a linguistic change.

Association within the Sentence

A quite different sort of association is that based upon the structure of a sentence, phrase, or word. One usually has a considerable part of a sentence shaped in his mind before he begins to speak. As he proceeds, the several parts of the sentence come successively into the focus of consciousness; but at any given moment the words already spoken, although they have passed out of the focus, are still present in the fringe of consciousness where they are gradually fading away, and the parts of the sentence which are yet to be uttered are gradually becoming more distinct in preparation for their emergence into the focus. One or another of these may rise into the focus out of its proper turn and interfere with the sound then being uttered.

The most common occurrence of this kind is the anticipation of a word or syllable or sound which belongs later in the sentence. Bawden reports many such cases. A person intended to say "spring chicken, ten cents a pound," but anticipation of the *t* of "ten" changed "chicken" into "ticken." Other examples are "put my coat in your pocket" for "put my cup in your coat-pocket," "praying on the street" for "playing on the street." Meringer reports among many others the lapse *das instruirte—konstruirte Instrument;* the speaker

intended to say *das konstruirte Instrument*, but the
second main word interfered with the first and altered
its initial syllable; he then detected his mistake and
corrected it before completing his sentence. Oertel reports "it outveighs in value" for "it outweighs in value."

The forms which appear in the other Indo-European
languages would lead one to expect English "four" and
German *vier* to begin with *h*. The labial spirant which
we actually find comes from the following numeral,
English "five," German *fünf*. Similarly, the Latin
word for "nine" ought to be **noven*, with the same
nasal that appears in *nonus*, but the anticipation of
decem changed **noven* to *novem*. Such changes as these
and the converse alteration of a numeral under the
influence of the one before it bear witness to the frequency of counting among primitive people who do not
understand the simple arithmetical processes.

When one word interferes with another, the sounds
which come into conflict usually stand under the same
accentual conditions. In "spring chicken, ten cents a
pound," the interfering sounds, *ch* and *t*, are the initials
of the most emphatic syllables of the sentence. In *das
konstruirte Instrument*, *kon-* and *In-* have the secondary
accent of their respective words. In "it outweighs in
value," *w* and *v* are initial consonants of accented syllables, and the same holds true of the interfering sounds
of the numerals "four" and "five." In *novem* and
decem the conflicting nasals are final consonants of
unaccented syllables.

Sounds which are contiguous or separated by only a
few other sounds may interfere with each other, even
though they do not stand under the same accentual

conditions.　Bawden cites "has the belly been passed?"
"belly" is "jelly" with interference by the initial of
the next word.　Of great linguistic importance is the
assimilation of contiguous consonants.　The compound
"cupboard" was once pronounced as it is spelled; after
the first vowel the vocal chords ceased to vibrate as the
lips were closed for the *p*-sound, the closure was maintained a moment, and then the vocal chords began to
vibrate as the lips were opened.　But some speaker
anticipated the voice which is proper to *b* while he was
closing the lips for *p;* and so he pronounced a double *b*.
Modern pronunciation simplifies the double consonant.
The assimilation seen in Latin *appono* for *adpono* is a
little more complicated in the muscular changes involved.
The original sound-group consisted of a closure of the
mouth passage in the *d*-position while the vocal chords
were vibrating, then a closure of the lips, a relaxation
of the *d*-contact, and finally an opening of the lips without accompanying voice.　When the *d* was assimilated
both the closure of the lips and the cessation of voice
were anticipated.　The change of *inmitto* to *immitto*
involved merely the anticipation of the lip closure of *m*,
while the change of *opmitto* to *ommitto* involved the
anticipation of voice and of the opening of the nasal
passage.

In these cases the assimilation results in the virtual
identity of the two consonants.　Frequently only some
characteristic of the second consonant is anticipated, as
when a voiced consonant before an unvoiced consonant
loses its vocal quality, or an unvoiced consonant before
a voiced consonant becomes voiced.　When **opduco*
became *obduco*, the only change was that the vocal

chords began to vibrate for *d* during the closure of the
lips for *p*.

Less frequently a consonant partially assimilates a
preceding vowel. Latin *novus* is the same word as
Greek νεός (originally νεϝός), and so *novus* was once
*nevos. A comparison with Gothic *niun* shows that the
Latin word for "nine" changed from **neven* to *novem;*
in both of these words *ev* became *ov*. The consonant
w (Latin *v*) involves two partial closures of the mouth
passage, one with the lips and the other between the
surface of the tongue and the soft palate. The vowel *o*
involves a lesser degree of closure a little farther forward
in the mouth and also a slight closure of the lips. The
vowel *e*, on the other hand, is a front vowel without
closure of the lips. A change of *e* to *o* before the consonant *w* is therefore a partial assimilation.

The assimilation of one vowel to another is most
easily studied in the case where they are separated by
one or more consonants. In nearly all of Meringer's
examples the two sounds have similar accentuation; he
reports interference between vowels which stand in contiguous syllables with different accent only in a few
lapses such as *viellaucht* for *vielleicht auch* and *hat soch*
for *hat sich doch*. Bawden reports "accustim" for "ac-
custom him."[1]

At an early stage in the history of the West Germanic
languages (English, German, Dutch, etc.) unaccented
vowels exerted a widespread influence over the accented
vowels of the initial syllables. In particular the vowel
i in inflectional endings and suffixes tended to convert

---

[1] Many scholars include such examples as these under *haplology*,
but I prefer to restrict that term as explained on p. 54.

back vowels into front or intermediate vowels. In Old High German the plural of *lamb* is *lembir*. Anglo-Saxon exhibits the modern contrast between "long" and "length" in the equivalent *lang* and *lengðu*, the latter of which was originally **lang-iþa*. In Anglo-Saxon the plural ending *-iz* of consonant stems was lost before our earliest documents were written, but we still see traces of it in such plurals as "men" from prehistoric **manniz* and "feet" from prehistoric **fōtiz*.

The assimilative influence which was exerted by Latin *v* (that is, *w*) in *novem* from **neven* is more often exerted by the vowel *u* in a following syllable. Avestan *vohu* comes from **vahu* (Sanskrit *vasu*), and *mosu* from **masu* (Sanskrit *makṣū*). In Anglo-Saxon *u* converted a preceding front vowel into a diphthong; beside Gothic *miluks* Anglo-Saxon has *mioluc* "milk," and **sefum*, the primitive Germanic word for "seven," appears in Anglo-Saxon as *seofon*.

Complete assimilation of a vowel to a following vowel is seen in Latin *rutundus* for *rotundus* and in the epigraphical *Sabastianus* and *vixillo* for *Sebastianus* and *vexillo*. Of the countless examples in Greek inscriptions and papyri we may cite ἥμυσυ for ἥμισυ in many Attic inscriptions.

It is not easy to detect cases of the assimilation of vowels in contact, for contraction usually results immediately. If, as many scholars assume, assimilation is a necessary preliminary to the contraction of unlike vowels into a monophthong, we must conclude that Latin *plantes* (subjunctive) from **plantāyēs* passed through the stage **planteēs*, and that Anglo-Saxon *nā* (English "no") came from *ne-ā through an intermediate stage *na-ā. Parallel cases are common in every language.

Just as a sound soon to be pronounced tends to be anticipated, so a sound already spoken tends to be **repeated**. The psychological process is almost the same, but the result upon language is different, and the phenomenon is less frequent. The instances may be grouped in the same way as those of anticipation.

Meringer reports many cases of the alteration of a word by a preceding word in the same sentence, for example, *Durch den Wald führt ein schöner Wag* (that is, *Weg*). A numeral may be affected by a preceding one; several Greek dialects have ὀκτώ "eight" and ἐννέα "nine" with the rough breathing of ἑπτά "seven." Assimilation of a consonant to another immediately preceding it is much less common than the progressive assimilation already discussed. Latin *pello* is from *pelno (cf. Greek πίλναμαι). The Greek name Πολυδεύκης became in Latin first *Polduces* and then *Polluces* (whence *Pollux*). Latin *sallo* "I salt" was originally *saldo, as is shown by the *t* of English "salt." In Oscan and Umbrian *nd* became *nn*, as in the Oscan gerundive *úpsannam* (*faciendam*). Plautus' *dispennite* and *distennite* for *dispendite* and *distendite* remind us that he was born in the Umbrian town of Sarsina. Assimilation of a consonant to a preceding consonant is seen in the Anglo-Saxon preterite *grētte* from *grēt-de, and partial assimilation in *īecte* from *īec-de. Partial assimilation is regular in the English plural suffix, which is *s* after voiceless consonants ("lips"), but *z* after voiced consonants ("ears").

In Latin a short vowel before a single consonant regularly appears as *i* (with certain exceptions) in any

syllable except the first and last of a word; but the
vowel of the initial syllable has assimilated that of the
second syllable in *alacer, elementum, vegetus*, and some
other words. An Attic inscription of the fourth century
B.C. shows Σίβιλλα for Σίβυλλα. Quite frequently the
assimilative influence comes from both directions, as in
English "woman" from early English *wimman* (Anglo-
Saxon *wífman*), whose first vowel has been altered
chiefly by the consonants preceding and following; that
the vowel of the second syllable was also of some influence is shown by the vowel of the plural "women"
(pronounced "wimin").

When two sounds or groups of sounds interfere with
each other, the result is sometimes an exchange of places,
a process which has long been called **metathesis** in our
grammars. Here again most of Meringer's examples
fall under the case where the two sounds stand under
similar accentual conditions, for example, *But und Glut*
for *Gut und Blut, und damin bit ich einig* for *und damit bin
ich einig*. He admits, however, that *b* and *g* sometimes
suffer metathesis when they belong to syllables of different accentuation, as in *gebinnt* for *beginnt, Begrauch* for
Gebrauch, etc. Several others of his examples are of the
same character, although he seems not to be aware of the
fact, for example, *die Callaverie* for *die Cavallerie, Prular*
for *Plural, Fraumeirer* for *Freimaurer*. Bawden records
many examples of both types. The interfering sounds
stand under similar accentuation in "feak and weeble"
for "weak and feeble," "the water the wetter" for
"the wetter the water," "plotoprasm" for "proto-
plasm." The accentual circumstances of the transposed
sounds differ in "ennaxation" for "annexation," "doni-

moes" for "dominoes," "regural" for "regular,"
"evelate" for "elevate," and a number of others. In
nearly all of his cases, however, as in all of Meringer's,
we have metathesis of sounds which are not immediately
contiguous.

That two consonants in contact may suffer metathesis is shown by one of Bawden's examples: "wist"
for "wits." Similar instances that have become usual
speech-forms are seen in Anglo-Saxon *axian* beside
ascian, whence dialectic Modern English "ax" beside the
normal "ask." Similarly, Latin *ascia* "ax" is related to
Greek ἀξίνη. French *fixe*, *taxe*, *sexe* become *fisque*,
tasque, *sesque* in the dialect of Paris. Metathesis of a
vowel and a consonant is seen in Chaucer's *brid* for
"bird" (which had a full vowel in Chaucer's time), and
in many Greek words such as Cretan Ἀφορδίτα for
Ἀφροδίτη and Homer's ἀταρπός beside Attic ἀτραπός.
Sometimes metathesis simply moves a sound out of its
position, as in "maganóli" for "magnolia," a mispronunciation of a child of six years, and in Bawden's
"disintregation" and "standsone." Of the same nature
is *Prancatius* for *Pancratius* on a Latin inscription, and
Syracusan Greek δρίφος for δίφρος. In Latin *cocodrillus*
for *crocodillus* a sound is displaced in the other direction.

We have noted that cases of associative interference
which are not repeated or imitated, such as those
observed by Meringer, usually concern sounds which
stand under similar accentual conditions. Now the
cases which become permanent features of a language
almost as regularly concern neighboring sounds. The
explanation seems to be this: since an accentual group
commonly embraces a whole word or several words, an

interference between sounds of similar accentual relations usually involves two or more words, and therefore cannot recur until the same combination of words occurs again. An interference between neighboring sounds, on the other hand, usually involves only one word, and may therefore recur whenever the word is spoken. So, although changes of the second sort are far less common than the others, each one of them is more likely to be repeated and hence to find imitators.

The phenomena of anticipation and repetition (compare pages 44–49) seem to be reversed in the somewhat less common process which is called **dissimilation**. There are four cases to be distinguished, the fourth of which is essentially different from the others:

1. Repetition of a sound or group of sounds is avoided (quite unintentionally, of course) by the suppression of one of the two occurrences. Meringer reports *hat Du's gesagt* for *hast Du's gesagt* and a great many similar lapses. Latin *vesti-spica* becomes *vesti-pica;* Greek δρύφρακτος becomes δρύφακτος, φρατρία becomes φατρία; German *Friedrich* becomes *Friedich.* An entire syllable is lost in "coborative" for "corroborative," a lapse reported by Bawden, and in Greek 'Απολλωφάνης for 'Απολλωνοφάνης.

2. Repetition is avoided by altering the sound in one of its two occurrences. From Meringer's half-dozen examples we select *ein grosser Gleu-* (immediately corrected by the speaker to *Greuel*). Latin *turtur* yields English "turtle-dove" and German *Turtel-taube;* the Latin suffix *alis* (*sacralis, principalis, nivalis*) appears as *aris* when appended to a base containing *l*, for example, *alaris, exemplaris, familiaris.* The dissimilation of

vowels is illustrated by *pêpi* for *pipi*, *mêma* for *mama*, and *pape* for *papa* in the speech of very young French children.[1]

3. Sometimes a regular sound-change is avoided if it would lead to the repetition of a sound. In Latin *ĕ*, *ă*, and *ŏ* before single consonants in medial syllables became *ĭ*, as in *reficio* beside *facio*. An intermediate stage in the change was *ĕ*, and this was retained when *i* preceded, *societas* (from **socio-tas*) beside *vicinitas; variegare* beside *purigare; aries, arietis* beside *miles, militis*. Original *ŏ* was retained after *u* in early Latin in such words as *mortuos* and *arguont*, although it had already become *u* in such words as *bonus* and *agunt*.

Dissimilation certainly belongs under the head of associative interference, for one of the sounds could not influence the other if they did not somehow get into consciousness at the same time. The exact manner of the interference, however, is not fully understood. Brugmann founds his explanation upon an involuntary reaction of the speaker which he calls *horror aequi*. This Latin name leaves the psychological process quite unexplained; and besides, certain facts indicate that there is no *horror aequi*. Extended alliterations have sometimes been admired; one may cite Ennius' lines:

O Tite tute Tati tibi tanta turanne tulisti,

and

Sóle luna lúce lucet álba leni láctea.

Even though modern taste condemns this as a poetic device, we find nothing difficult in the repetition of the sounds, and we can understand how they might give

[1] Reported by Grammont, *Mélanges Meillet*, 64; and Deville, *Rev. de linguistique*, XXIV, 10–15.

pleasure. But no one could find aesthetic pleasure or fail to find difficulty in the nonsense syllables: "Peter Piper picked a peck of pickled peppers; where is the peck of pickled peppers Peter Piper picked?" The trouble comes from the alternation of slightly dissimilar sounds—in this case, the voiceless mutes *p*, *t*, and *k*. In the sentence, "an old cold scold sold a school coal skuttle," the most difficult set of alternating sounds is *c*, *sc*, and *s*. To translate this into terms of the physiology of speech, it is easy to repeat a given articulation an indefinite number of times, but it is difficult to produce a succession of muscular co-ordinations which differ slightly from one another.

In pronouncing these cacophonous combinations the tendency is toward a further assimilation; we say "Peper Piper," "pickled peckers," or "scoal-skuttle." Apparently the tendency toward dissimilation arises only in case the interfering groups are of such a character as to make assimilation inconvenient. The assimilated form of *hast Du's gesagt?* would be *has gu's gesagt?* but this would introduce two unfamiliar forms into the sentence, and we shall see later that linguistic innovations tend to produce familiar sounds and combinations. The assimilated form of *societas* would be *socicitas* or *socititas*, either one of which would be easy to pronounce, but out of harmony with established linguistic habits; *socĭĭtas* would yield *socītas*, and that, too, would be a linguistic monstrosity.

4. The term **haplology** is sometimes applied to any dissimilative loss of a syllable, but we shall restrict its use to a certain group of cases which seem to differ psychologically from other kinds of dissimilation. If a

vowel stands between similar consonants or consonant groups, the vowel and one of the consonants or consonant groups tend to be lost, as when Latin *semimodius became *semodius*. The dissimilative character of the change is apparent; but the distinctive feature of haplology is that the consonant forms a sort of switch from one syllable to the next. In the following diagram (a modification of one in Oertel[1]) the capital letters indicate the sounds actually spoken, and the letter extending across both lines represents the sound which was common to both original syllables:

$$\text{SE}\underset{\text{ODIUS}}{\overset{\text{i-}}{M}}$$

A child intended to say "Post Toasties" (the name of a certain cereal preparation), but actually said "Posties." Our diagram stands:

$$\text{PO}\underset{\text{IES}}{\overset{\text{oa}}{ST}}$$

The process is obviously similar to the analogical changes which were discussed on page 38.

Other instances of haplology are Latin *nutrix* for *nutri-trix*, *scripsti* for *scripsisti*, *amatust* for *amatus est*, Greek ἡμέδιμνον for ἡμι-μέδιμνον, German *Superindent* for *Superintendent*. English "Gloucester" was once pronounced in three syllables, "Glousester," the second of which has been lost by haplology. Chaucer pronounced the adverb from the adjective "humble" in three syllables, *humblely*, while we say "humbly." Shakespeare's verse requires us to read "prevent it"

[1] *Op. cit.*, p. 208.

as "prevent'." One often hears the pronunciation "libry" for "library" and "probly" for "probably."

Rhythm

One of the most fundamental facts of human nature is the sense of rhythm, which results in large part from the swinging motion of legs and arms. "The four limbs," says Titchener,[1] "are, so to speak, four pendulums attached to the trunk of the body. As we run or walk the legs swing alternately, and with each leg swings the arm on the opposite side." Particularly important for our purpose is the auditory rhythm which may be observed in pure form by listening to the ticking of a clock; although all the beats may be precisely alike, we hear them in groups: "tick tock, tick tock" or "tick tock, tick tock; tick tock, tick tock." Very commonly the tactual rhythm of walking is associated with the auditory rhythm of our footfalls.

The importance of rhythm in poetry is too familiar to require comment, and all readers of this book are aware that there is much regularity of rhythm in artistic prose.[2] The rhythmic modulation of even the simplest speech may be seen by analyzing a bit of conversation taken at random from Mark Twain's *Tom Sawyer*. Musical notation is used for convenience, in spite of the fact that speech is too flexible to fit a mathematical scheme. Although in some instances the time indicated is only approximately correct, the intervals of time between accents are virtually the same throughout.

[1] *Primer of Psychology*, p. 113.
[2] For a scientific treatment of this subject, see W. M. Patterson, *The Rhythm of Prose*.

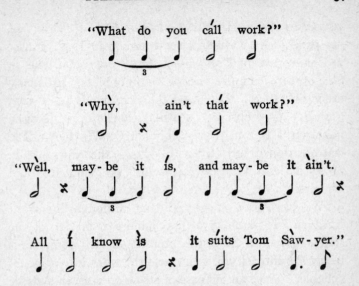

The dynamic character of stress-rhythm appears quite clearly in such pairs of words as "transpórt" and "trànsportátion," "corróborate" and "corròborátion"; the fixed accent of the suffix -átion induces a secondary accent on the second or third syllable preceding and sometimes, as in our first example, on a syllable which in the primitive is unaccented. Similarly, the initial accent of German *Vórurteil*[1] inverts the accent of the second member of the compound (*Úrteil*). The tendency appears even more impressively in longer compounds, such as *Reàlschulóberlèhrer*. Similar phenomena may sometimes be observed in the phrase. A number of Swedish and Danish dissyllables have the accent on the final syllable, except when they stand before an accented syllable, for example, Swedish *kusín*,

---

[1] The secondary accent of this word is very weak, but there seems to be no doubt of its position on the final syllable.

but *kùsin Ánna;* Danish *Emíl,* but *Èmil Hánsen.* At
one time such a variation was common in English also;
in Chaucer we find *cosýn,* but *còsyn mýn,* etc., and in
Shakespeare "impúre" beside "ìmpure blóts," and many
other instances. Later poets occasionally use such
phrases as "òbscure deáth" (Shelley), "dèspised
mónarch" (Byron), "an òccult hínt" (Whittier). The
last-mentioned adjective still shows the variation in
prose, at least in America, as also do "contrite" and
"inverse."

We have seen (page 22) that although the word
"heaven" is normally a dissyllable a reduction of the
stress of *n* until the total intensity of that sound falls
below the intensity of *v* converts the word into a mono-
syllable. Since an increase of stress on a given syllable
usually induces a diminution of stress on neighboring
syllables, a strong stress-accent tends to suppress
unaccented syllables whose most sonorous sound is a
consonant. The weakened consonant may attach
itself to the accented syllable, as in the case of "heav'n,"
but quite as often it goes with a neighboring unaccented
syllable. The second syllable of "generally" has no
vowel, but in careful, deliberate pronunciation we make
the sonorous consonant *r* carry the syllable ("gén-ŗ-ļ-y").
When we speak more rapidly the stress on the first
syllable reduces the stress of *r* until its intensity falls
below that of the following sound, and we say "gén-rļ-y."

A strong stress-accent also tends to reduce the
sonorousness of unaccented vowels, a process which is
called vowel-weakening. In prehistoric Latin there was
a stress-accent on the initial syllable of every word,
and it was this accent which changed ă to ĕ and then

(before single consonants) to *ĭ*, as in *abigo* beside *ago* and *reficio* beside *facio*. By degrees the most sonorous of the vowels changed to one of the least sonorous under the influence of stress on a neighboring syllable.

Frequently a heavy stress-accent leads to the loss of unaccented vowels. Latin has many such "syncopated" forms as *repperi* from **ré-peperi*, *iunior* from **iúvenior*, *pergo* from **pér-rego*. Sometimes when a vowel is lost in this way a sonorous consonant prevents the syllable from being lost. English "vocálic" has a vowel in the second syllable, but in "vòcalizátion" the accent on the first syllable causes the vowel of the second syllable to be lost and leaves *l* as the most sonorous sound in its syllable. A further reduction of stress in rapid speech causes the loss of the syllable, "vò-cli-zá-tion."

The rhythmic tendency of pitch-accent is scarcely less strong than that of stress-accent. Even in a language which makes as little of pitch as English, speech in a monotone is exceedingly disagreeable and quite rare. Our pitch, like that of French and German, is chiefly a function of the sentence; we vary the pitch of individual words almost at will.

In many languages the pitch of particular words and syllables is as definitely fixed as their stress is in English. In Chinese and some other languages a variation in pitch, even though the sound be otherwise unchanged, is felt to produce a new word which is capable of carrying an entirely different meaning. Even where there is a relatively fixed system of pitch-accent, alterations are made under the influence of the rhythmic tendency, for example, Greek σῶμά τε: λόγος τε (*sômá tè: lógòs te*). As far as we know, pitch-accent does not exert any influence upon the quality or quantity of vowels or consonants.

That the rhythmic tendency applies to quantity as well as to accent is shown by the quantitative verse of Greek, Latin, and many other languages and also by the quantitative rhythm of artistic classical prose. In most of the Greek and Roman authors, to be sure, we find few variations from the normal quantity for metrical purposes, except in foreign words and proper names. In Homer, however, such variation is frequent (for example ἐνί:εἰνί Θύρῃσι), and it has been plausibly suggested[1] that in early Greek this was a feature of ordinary speech. Some scholars assume such variation in the Indo-European parent-speech to account for pairs like ἐλαφρότερος:σοφώτερος, δουλοσύνη:ἱερωσύνη, and the Sanskrit reduplicated aorists açiçriyam : ajījanam.

In languages such as English, which have a strong stress-accent, quantitative rhythm is so largely dominated by accentual rhythm that it can hardly be studied separately; nearly all unaccented vowels have been shortened.

Speed of Utterance

We have seen that an increase in the speed of utterance increases the effect of a stress-accent. The reason for this is that when we speak rapidly we have less time for making the complicated nervous and muscular adjustments that are necessary to the production of speech-sounds, and so some of the movements are incomplete, inexact, or ill-timed; we are more likely to make mistakes when we speak rapidly. Probably this applies

---

[1] Van Ginneken, *Principes de linguistique psychologique*, pp. 300 f.

in varying degrees to nearly all sorts of mispronunciation; certainly it has an important connection with the phenomena of assimilation and dissimilation, as one discovers by reciting the syllables about Peter Piper at varying rates of speed.

Rapidity of utterance is not an independent cause of sound-change, but only a re-enforcing cause. An increase in speed is related to sound-change much as a reduction of vitality is related to disease: both reduce the patient's powers of resistance, but neither can induce a particular malady. The analogy is not perfect, however; Meringer[1] has not been able to detect a greater liability to mispronunciation in speakers of rapid utterance than in those whose rate of speech is slower. No doubt habitually rapid speech goes parallel with unusual speed and accuracy in making nervous and muscular co-ordinations; whether the habit or the skill is the cause of the other is a question for a psychologist to answer.

Ease of Articulation

Many of the changes we have discussed result in an easier articulation; it is easier to say "cub*rd*" than "cup-board," *Polluces* than *Polduces*, *exemplaris* than **exemplalis*, *semodius* than **semimodius*, *repperi* than **repeperi*. Many sound-changes also among those that we have not mentioned simplify articulation. A monophthong requires less muscular and nervous energy than a diphthong (Latin *ae* became *e;* Greek *αι* became *e*); a spirant is a less complicated sound than an aspirate (Indo-European *ph* became Latin *f;* *φ* was pronounced

---

[1] *Aus dem Leben der Sprache*, p. 122.

ph, as in "hap-hazard," in ancient Greek, but is now pronounced *f*); the loss of a sound saves effort unless the resulting combination of sounds is difficult to articulate (Latin *v* was lost between like vowels, Greek *ϝ* was lost in all positions in some dialects). It seems probable, then, that in many cases the greater ease with which a new sound is produced is a contributing factor in its first production.

Such a tendency is not always present, for changes in the reverse direction are not uncommon. Monophthongs sometimes become diphthongs, as in English *ā* and *ō* have become *āy* and *ōw* (for example, "pay," "grow"). In the first Germanic mutation of consonants *t* became *th* (Latin *tenuis*, English "thin"); this *th* under certain circumstances became *d* (Latin *centum*, English "hundred"); original *d*, however, became *t* (Latin *duo*, English "two"). These changes did not all take place at the same time, and they were more complicated than this summary statement would indicate; but the fact remains that original *t* sometimes became English *d*, while original *d* regularly became English *t*. Not all of the changes concerned can possibly be due to a tendency toward ease of articulation.

Indeed we cannot often say that any simple sound is easier than another; for no language makes common use of a sound which seems difficult to the speakers of that language. We should not invoke the tendency to avoid effort as a cause of any sound-changes except those which clearly result in the omission or simplification of muscular movement.

In one case this tendency seems to operate quite regularly. If *i* or *u* is immediately followed by a dissimilar vowel, a consonantal glide is developed between them (unless the *i* or *u* itself becomes consonantal with loss of a syllable). Since *i* and *u* are less sonorous than the other vowels, the speaker can produce the decrease of intensity which marks the syllable division between *i* and *a*, for example, only by a considerable decrease in stress at the close of the *i*-sound. If the sonorousness of the *i* is decreased at the same time, the change in stress need not be so great; but when *i* becomes less sonorous the result is *y*.

Many consonant groups involve an exact co-ordination of muscular processes. In order to produce the group *sl* one must close the *s*-aperture between the tip of the tongue and the gum and at the same moment open the *l*-apertures between the sides of the tongue and the gum. If the former adjustment precedes, the result is a complete closure between the tongue and the gum in the *t*-position, and when this is relaxed by the opening of the *l*-apertures we hear the explosion which constitutes the sound of *t*, as when English "scarcely" is pronounced "scarcetly." Conversely, the group *stl* requires that the closure of the *s*-aperture shall precede the opening of the *l*-apertures. If this is not done, the *t*-explosion is omitted, as when "beastly" is pronounced "beasly" (the familiar pronunciation in England). Other unstable consonant groups are seen in "stream" from Indo-European *sreu*, "ches(t)nut," Latin *sum(p)si* and *sum(p)tus*. In such cases we find changes in both directions ("scarcetly" : "beasly"). Other consonant combinations which involve exactly timed changes of articulation are broken up by the development of a vowel, as when English "elm" and "Henry" become "elum" and "Henery," or early Latin *periclum* and *vehiclum* become *periculum* and *vehiculum*.

In the cases mentioned in the last paragraph the only difficulty is that of making a movement at precisely the right moment. That, however, is not really a difficult thing to do when once it has become habitual. The development or loss of a *t* between *s* and *l* and of a vowel between *l* and *m* does not really result in greater ease of articulation unless those combinations are uncommon in the language concerned, or the speaker who makes the change is just learning the language. In these cases, then, we should not speak of a tendency toward ease of articulation, but of a tendency to eliminate unfamiliar sounds or groups of sounds.

Loan-words are peculiarly subject to this tendency; just as those who learn a foreign language tend to substitute familiar sounds for the unfamiliar foreign sounds, so the borrowers of a foreign word adapt it to their own phonetic habits. When German *Walz* made its way into English, the unfamiliar initial sound of the German was displaced by English *v* or *w*, the latter of which has become usual on account of the identity of the written character with the German letter.

Unfamiliar combinations arise occasionally in the development of a language, and then are eliminated; the Greek for "seventh" should be ἕβδμος, but we find ἕβδομος in some dialects, ἕβδεμος in others.

The tendency to avoid unfamiliar sounds often combines with other factors in producing a sound-change; when Latin **is-pse* became *ipse* an unfamiliar combination was eliminated by dissimilation. The German name *Schlesinger* is often pronounced with metathesis

Sleshinger in America, where the initial combination *shl* is unfamiliar. "Aeroplane" becomes "airioplane," chiefly by analogy with "air," partly by metathesis, and partly also because *aë* is an unfamiliar combination in English.

Spelling and Pronunciation

In cultivated languages spelling frequently leads to a change in pronunciation. The French word *faute* was adopted in Middle English and was pronounced nearly as in French for some time. At length some schoolmaster noticed the connection with Latin *fallo* and heralded his discovery by spelling the word with an *l*. Presently some other pedant pronounced the *l* thus introduced, and now we all follow his example. The English names "Norwich" and "Greenwich" (pronounced "Norij," "Grinij") have been given to several American towns, but here they are usually pronounced as spelled. Although the *t* of "often" has been silent in normal speech for two centuries, many persons, misled by the spelling, now take great pains to pronounce it.

Custom and Pronunciation

The habits and ideals of different human groups differ widely. Laborers of some races habitually sing at their work, but other laborers would consider such a practice the height of folly. In some communities all decent women wear rings in their noses, in others in the lower lips, and in still others in the ears, while some communities regard a ring attached to any part of the head as a badge, not of respectability, but of the reverse. In one land it is proper to express emotion as fully as possible by gesture, facial expression, and tone of voice; but in another, people try to appear as if they had no emotions at all.

Many linguistic facts must be connected with such social habits. It has been suggested that the comparative lack of facial expression in England is a cause of the weak articulation of the labials which is prevalent there. Perhaps the loss of pitch-accent in many highly cultured languages is in part due to the civilized habit of hiding emotions. A rather slovenly fashion of closing the mouth before one has quite finished what he is saying yields vulgar English "nope" for "no" and "yep" for "yea." If the final sound is *s*, the premature closure is in the *t*-position, and the result is "acrosst," "sincet," "clost," "oncet," etc. No doubt it will some day be possible to detect other and clearer cases of the influence of custom upon speech.

Unknown Factors

No doubt there are other causes of primary change of sound, and further study will probably bring some of them to light. Something is to be hoped for from further collections of momentary lapses, such as those published by Meringer, and something also from the laboratories of phonetics and psychology.

In the meantime it would be well for linguists to study such changes of sound as recur independently in different languages. For example, *z* becomes *r* in West and North Germanic (Gothic *maiza*, English "more," German *mehr*, Swedish *mera*), in Latin and Umbrian (Oscan *ezum*, Latin *ero*, Umbrian *erom*), in certain Greek dialects (Eretrian ἔχουριν, Μίργος), in Sanskrit

(*sarvais tantraiḥ : sarvair guṇaiḥ*). If all similar phenomena from other known languages were compared
with these, the reason for the tendency might appear.
At present we can merely say that *z* and some types of *r*
are produced by similar articulations and that some
types of *r* require less expenditure of breath than is
needed to produce *z*.

CHAPTER III

SECONDARY CHANGE OF FORM

We have now to consider the spread of new forms over a greater or a smaller territory. Many innovations do not spread at all or even establish themselves at the spot where they originate. Some of them are detected by the speaker and corrected at once; others, which escape his notice, the hearer detects and mentally brands as mistakes. A great many phonetic changes do, however, gain currency, and this in two very different ways. Some changes establish themselves in hundreds of words, while others, such as that of Latin *nutritrix* to *nutrix*, are confined to a single word.

Changes Affecting Several Words

Changes of sound which are common to several words are among the most frequent linguistic changes, and they differ from all the others in that they are usually regular in their operation. Unless they are hindered by some opposing tendency, they usually apply, not to a few words, but to all those in which the sound occurs in similar surroundings.

Anglo-Saxon *āð* has become "oath," and with almost perfect regularity Anglo-Saxon accented *ā* in other words also has become *ō* (or, more accurately, *ōw*; see above, page 18). We have "own" from *āgan*, "bone" from *bān*, "goat" from *gāt*, "comb" from *cāmb*, "foam" from *fām*, "whole" from *hāl*, "home"

68

from *hām*, "moan" from *mān*, "sow" from *sāwan*, "token" from *tācen*, etc. These and many parallel instances are summarized in the formula: Anglo-Saxon accented *ā* became Modern English *ō* (or rather, *ōw*). Such a formula is called a **phonetic law.** There is another phonetic law to the effect that Indo-European *d* became Germanic *t*. It is based upon correspondences between the related idioms and the Germanic languages, such as these between the classical languages and English:

decem: "ten"	δέρω: "tear"
duo: "two"	*dens*: "tooth"
dicere: "teach"	*cordem*: "heart"
domare: "tame"	*sedere*: "sit"

The phonetic law that in Latin *s* between vowels became *r* (through the intermediate stage of *z*) is a formulaic statement of many such relationships as these:

genus: *generis*	*gestus*: *gero*
dis-tineo: *dir-imo*	*nefas*: *nefarius*

Roman grammarians record early Latin *meliosem*, *foedesum*, and *lases* for classical *meliorem*, *foederum*, and *lares*. We might multiply indefinitely examples of each of these phonetic laws.

We must carefully note, however, that phonetic laws operate only under certain conditions, or we shall not be able to trace their regularity. Although, as we have seen, Latin *ă* if originally unaccented became *ĭ*, many words show *ĕ* from *ă*. Contrast the second and fourth columns below.

facio:*inficio*   *factus*:*infectus*
capio:*incipio*   *captus*:*inceptus*
rapio:*deripio*   *raptus*:*dereptus*
ago:*adigo*   *pario*:*reperio*
habeo:*inhibeo*   *partus*:*repertus*
datus:*red-ditus*   *sacro*:*consecro*

The confusion disappears as soon as we recognize the
fact that the phonetic law in question operated only
before a single consonant other than *r*,[1] while before
double consonants and *r* unaccented *ă* became *ĕ*. To
put the matter in terms of historical development,
unaccented *ă* became *ĕ*, and then unaccented *ĕ* before
single consonants except *r* became *ĭ*. Similarly, Anglo-
Saxon *ā* changed to Modern English *ō* only when
accented; the regular development of Anglo-Saxon
unaccented *ā* is seen in "abide" from *ābídan*, "arise"
from *ārísan*. Again, Latin *s* became *r* only between
vowels. We have noticed *s* in *genus*, *distineo*, *gestus*,
and *nefas;* it occurs in a host of other words besides.

Phonetic laws operate regularly wherever they
operate at all, but they do not necessarily operate over
the entire territory of a language. In the greater part
of the United States *r* before a consonant is retained
in such words as "cart," "hard," "barn"; but in the
South, in a large part of New England, and in the city
of New York *r* in this position is lost with lengthening
of the preceding vowel. In most Greek dialects original
long *ā* remained, so that first-declension nouns ended in
that vowel as they do in Latin (ποινᾱ). In Attic and
Ionic, however, this sound became η, and so we have

---

[1] This is not a complete statement of the facts; but further details
are not necessary to our point.

first-declension nouns like ποίνη. In Attic alone another phonetic law gives ᾱ after ε, ι, and ρ, so that we find χώρα contrasting with Ionic χώρη.

Sometimes a phonetic law is confined to a particular class. In Southern England the lower classes have lost the sound *h*, but it is carefully retained by educated people. In New York City, before the New England loss of *r* before a consonant was introduced,[1] a part of the words concerned had suffered a different change in the language of the lower classes; the syllabic *r* of "bird," "third," "first," "hurt," "worm," etc., had developed into a diphthong whose first element is an abnormal vowel (see above, page 20) similar to German *ö* or French *eu* and whose second element is *i*. One can easily distinguish the native from the imported delivery boys and street-car conductors by the presence or absence of such pronunciations as "böid," "thöid," "föist," "höid," "wöim." Other local and class phonetic laws are illustrated by the western pronunciation "Americy," "Sary," "Nevady," etc., and by Cockney "lidy" ("laide") for "lady," and "roud" ("raud") for "road."

A phonetic law continues in force only for a limited time, and after it has once ceased to operate a sound fulfilling all the conditions for the change may come to exist in the language and remain unchanged. If Latin *causa* had had that form at the time when *s* between vowels was being changed to *r*, the classical word would

---

[1] My efforts to gather evidence on the history of *r* before a consonant in New York City have not been successful. I know, however, that *r* in that position was still pronounced in southwestern Connecticut fifty years ago. The change of *r̥* to *öi* must have antedated the loss of *r*. See also p. 77.

have been *caura;* but until the time of Augustus the
word was *caussa.* So also *caesus, rusus, misi, fusus,* and
others were pronounced with *ss* in the early period;
when at last *ss* became *s* in these words the phonetic
law had ceased to operate, and *s* between vowels persisted. Anglo-Saxon *sc* has become *sh* in "shin,"
"shirt," "shrew," "shriek," etc.; but nevertheless *sc*
(often spelled *sk*) is by no means uncommon in Modern
English. In fact we have numerous by-forms in *sk* of
words in *sh;* beside "ship" we have "skiff"; "shirt"
and "skirt" are historically the same word; and so
are "shriek" and "screech"; "shrew" and "screw"
(a skittish horse). The *sk* forms were borrowed from
other languages (chiefly Danish) after the change of
genuine English *sc* to *sh.*

Borrowed words, even when they do not have a form
that has previously existed in the borrowing language,
often produce apparent exceptions to a phonetic law.
In Modern English, beside "whole" from Anglo-Saxon
hāl, we have also the form "hale," which does not go
back to the Anglo-Saxon word, but to Danish *heel;* this
is cognate, to be sure, with the genuine English word,
but it acquired its peculiar form during its history as a
Danish word. The genuine Latin word corresponding
to English "red," Greek ἐρυθρός, Sanskrit *rudhirás,* is
ruber; Latin *rufus* is borrowed from another of the
Italic languages in which Indo-European *dh* in the
middle of a word became *f.*

It was the discovery of the regularity of the phonetic
laws that made possible the science of comparative
philology. As long as scholars thought, for example,
that original *dh* in the middle of a word might appear

in Latin as *b* or *f* indifferently there was no way of showing that *ruber* is the native Latin word and that *rufus*
is a loan-word; both might be genuine developments
of the same original stem. Furthermore, the fact that
dh initial appeared as *f* in Latin *fumus* (Greek θῦμα) and
in many other words did not prevent the connection of
deus and θεός on the assumption of an original initial *dh*.
The equation of English "deer" with Greek θήρ and
Latin *ferus* on the basis of assumed Indo-European *dh*
was for a long time a favorite etymology, in spite of the
fact that Aeolic Greek has φήρ instead of θήρ. Indeed,
it was possible to connect any two words of any two
languages by merely assuming a sufficient number of
sound-changes. Voltaire's sneering description of etymology as the science in which the consonants count
for little and the vowels for nothing continued to be
deserved for many years after the death of its author.
For some time after scholars began to speak of "phonetic
laws," they grouped under them only a part of the
material and then added a chapter on "sporadic change,"
in which they discussed what they thought to be exceptions to the phonetic laws. Sometimes they set up two
contradictory phonetic laws, either of which might
operate, it was supposed, in any given case.

As linguistic knowledge broadened and deepened,
scholars came gradually to recognize the prevailing
regularity of phonetic change, and to feel more and more
skepticism in regard to "sporadic change." The
climax of thirty years of increasing strictness in the
treatment of sound-changes came in 1876, when Leskien,
in an essay entitled *Die Deklination im Slavisch-
Litauischen und Germanischen*, advanced the theory

that phonetic laws have no exceptions, except those which can be accounted for by the intervention of other phonetic laws or by some analogical influence. The matter was vigorously debated for many years, and the outcome of the discussion, for the present at least, is a compromise. Few scholars now deny the possibility of exceptions to the phonetic laws, but in practice all reputable linguists assume that these laws are regular, and all refrain from advancing etymologies which violate them.

Although phonetic laws are usually regular in their operation, it is not hard to find cases where they are more or less vacillating. English $\overline{oo}$ has been shortened to $\breve{oo}$ in "book" and "good." Many speakers in various parts of the English-speaking world habitually shorten the sound in certain other words, such as "room," "cooper," "roof," "proof," "spoon," "food," "soot," and "root." In a third group of words $\overline{oo}$ is never shortened, for example, "fool," "moon," "Susan," "shoe." There is inconsistency in standard English between the first group and the other two, while with regard to the treatment of words of the second group one can find all imaginable differences between speakers. In the dialect of New England $\bar{o}$ is changed to the u of "but" in certain words. The shortened form is very common in "stun" for "stone" and the phrase "to hum" for "at home," and it is heard in many other words also, but in different words in different localities. Latin mn is treated in no less than four different ways. In *femina*, *nominalis*, and *guminasium* for Greek γυμνάσιον, an epenthetic vowel appears. In most words the group remains unchanged in standard Latin. In the language of the streets *mn* is sometimes assimilated to *nn*, as in *alonnus* for *alumnus* and *lanna* for *lamna*, while sometimes *p* is developed between the two nasals, as in *dampnum* for *damnum*, *calumpnia* for *calumnia*, *solempnis* for *solemnis*.

Writers on scientific grammar try to explain away such irregularities by assigning the various sounds to different class or local dialects, by making them represent different chronological stages of a continuous development, or by pointing out the phonetic surroundings under which each one appears. Such procedure is entirely proper, and it has reduced numerous apparent irregularities to order. There remain, however, many cases which cannot be explained away.

We have record of temporary vacillation between rival pronunciations followed by the complete victory of one of them. In Shakespeare's time "war" rhymed with "far," "warm" with "harm," "wanting" with "granting." In the eighteenth century the modern pronunciation of such words was the common one, but many people kept the old sound *ah* (Continental *a*) in certain words, as "wart," "dwarf," "wabble," "wad," "wallop." For the last hundred years or so the standard English pronunciation has consistently employed the sound-group *waw* for earlier *wah;* whereas the change was irregular in the eighteenth century, it was regular in the nineteenth. In American English the irregularity still persists; most of us say *ah* in the words "wabble," "wad," and "wallop"; many of us, in "wash"; and some of us, in "water." Probably American English will eventually work its way to uniformity, as the English of the mother-country has already done.

Sometimes a period of vacillation is followed by the victory of the original sound. In Latin there was at one time a tendency to lengthen short vowels before *gn*. It seems certain that people said *dīgnus, sīgnum, īgnis,* as well as *dĭgnus, sĭgnum, ĭgnis,* although for some words, such as *magnus,* there is no evidence of a lengthened pronunciation. But even for the words first mentioned the inherited forms of the Romance languages and the borrowed forms of the Germanic and Celtic languages show that the pronunciation with a short vowel finally prevailed. In this case the net result of the incipient change was to leave things as they were at first.

Sound-changes sometimes start in a particular part of a linguistic community and gradually spread, as waves radiate from a pebble dropped into a body of water. Sound-changes, however, need not spread in concentric circles; they may move rapidly in some directions, slowly in others, and not at all in still others.

A change of this sort which has been much studied is the so-called second or High German mutation of consonants, which caused the difference between the consonants of such English and German words as "two" and *zwei,* "foot" and *Fuss,* "sheep" and *Schaf,* "daughter" and *Tochter,* "brother" and *Bruder.* These changes began about 600 A.D. in South Germany and spread gradually northward. As the tendency to shift the mutes moved farther from the starting-point, it became weaker and affected fewer sounds. The northern districts were almost untouched by it. Most remarkable of all, the change spread across dialect borders without interruption, while, on the other hand, the

Frankish dialect was only partially covered; thence-forth we have High Frankish, which took part in the change, and Low Frankish, which did not.

Another gradually spreading sound-change may be observed in the neighborhood of New York City just now. In a large part of New England *r* before a consonant is mute in such words as "cart," "hard," "first," "horde," and this pronunciation is gradually spreading to the southwest. Fifty years ago, I have been informed, it had not reached Greenwich, Connecticut. At present the boundary follows the New England line nearly to the coast, then it swerves westward to the Hudson, and presently moves westward again to include several of the Jersey suburbs. Along the Jersey shore directly opposite the city the natives as well as the commuters pronounce in this respect precisely as the city people do. A little farther back, in Hackensack and Newark, both pronunciations may be heard; the boundary runs through these towns and the change has not worked out to uniformity there. There is little doubt that soon the whole district tributary to New York City will pronounce "caht," etc.

The most remarkable and most important sound-changes are those which are regular in their operation. For many years students of language have devoted much time to discovering, describing, and tabulating phonetic laws; no other group of linguistic phenomena has been more extensively or more profitably studied. Many attempts have been made to account for their regularity, and some factors in the problem have been recognized; but there is not today any generally accepted theory of sound-change. We shall consider two ways in which

regular changes of form occur. It is very probable that
these two factors sometimes co-operate, and there may
be other factors in the problem.

Many sound-changes, as we have seen, do not
originate in a sudden and violent change, such as might
be inferred from our formulation of the phonetic laws.
Our grammars say that Latin unaccented *a* before a
single consonant became *i*. But in reality we know that
a was not changed directly into *i;* there was certainly
an intermediate stage *e*, and probably there were many
other intermediate stages. The weakening of unaccented *a* was induced by the strong stress-accent of
early Latin, an influence which must constantly have
affected all speakers. Every time anyone pronounced
a word like **réfacio* he tended to make the second vowel
a little closer and less sonorous than before; the change,
however, was very slight in each case and therefore
did not attract attention or provoke correction. Nevertheless each new stage on the road from *a* to *i* must
have served as a point of departure for another change
in the same direction.

A sound-change may be made regular in this way,
whenever one of the causes of primary change of sound
operates upon all the speakers of a community, provided
the change in question is capable of proceeding by
imperceptible stages. A change of social customs, such
as an increase in the size of ornamental rings worn in the
upper lip, or a fashion of splitting the upper lip, or a
habit of keeping the lips closed as much as possible,
would certainly produce regular changes in some of the
speech-sounds. If a whole community adopts a new
language, there is a consistent tendency to modify the

sounds of the new language in the direction of the familiar sounds of the old.

But there are many phonetic laws whose regularity cannot be thus explained. Some changes cannot take place by imperceptible stages; for example, the change of *qu* to *p* in several languages (Oscan *pod* is from *quod*), or the change of *tl* to *cl* in Latin (*pōc[u]lum* is from **pōtlom*). Even some changes which might take place by imperceptible stages are nevertheless observed to involve at certain times an easily perceptible variation between words or between speakers; for example, the eighteenth-century inconsistency between "warm" rhyming with "form" and "wart" rhyming with "part," and the present inconsistency in the pronunciation of "room," etc. Even in case we cannot disprove that a change took place by slow degrees, we are usually unable to point out any persistent cause of the tendency to change in the given direction. It is probable that we should assign an important rôle to the second method by which changes of form are known to become regular.

In the dialect of Missouri and the neighboring states, final *a* in such words as "America," "Arizona," "Nevada," becomes *y*—"Americy," "Arizony," "Nevady." All educated people in that region carefully correct this vulgarism out of their speech; and many of them carry the correction too far and say "Missoura," "praira," etc. That plain soldier, the emperor Vespasian, had the vulgar habit of saying *ō* for *au*, and, says Suetonius, a courtier named Florus once cautioned him to say *plaustra* instead of *plostra;* next morning the imperial pupil greeted his instructor as "Flaurus." Suetonius records this as one of Vespasian's jests; but

many Romans changed *ō* to *au* in the mere effort to
speak correctly, as in *scauria* for Greek σκωρία in an
inscription. Such over-corrections are common in all
languages.[1] For the native of Missouri the attempt to
say "America," "Arizona," and "Nevada" is an attempt
to substitute for his native *y* the more elegant sound *a*.
The feeling inevitably arises that final *y* is wrong and
should be changed to *a;* this feeling has actually led
to the pronunciations "Missoura" and "praira," and it
might easily lead to the conversion of every final *y* to *a*.

Such a spread of a sound-change from word to word
closely resembles analogical change; the chief difference
is that in analogical change the association groups are
based upon meaning, while in this case the groups
are based upon form. We may illustrate with the
change of initial *en-* to *in-* in Latin. For reasons which
we need not now consider, *ě* before the velar nasal
(English *ng*) became *ĭ*, and consequently words and
phrases containing the preposition **en* (cognate with
Greek ἐν) or the negative prefix **en* (cognate with
Greek α privative) before a velar consonant changed
the initial vowel to *ĭ;* **enclaudo* became *includo* and
*encoctus became *incoctus*. By analogy the preposition
and the negative prefix became *in*, even when other
sounds followed, and so we have *infero, ineo, inutilis,
in arce*, etc.[2] The preposition **en* was closely associated

[1] Cf. Wheeler, *Transactions of the American Philological Association*, XXXII, 5-15.

[2] It is possible that in the case of the preposition, weakening in unaccented syllables may have contributed a few forms with *ĭ*; but one should
remember that in prehistoric Latin a compound like *inicio* and probably a phrase like *in arce* had the accent on the first syllable. It is also
possible that assimilation to a following *i* may have contributed some
forms like *inicio*.

with the compound preposition *endo* (cognate with English "into"), which had the same meaning, and it was also associated with the prepositions **enter* and **enfra;* analogy changed these to *indu, inter,* and *infra.* Now this extensive change of initial *en-* to *in-* might have induced a feeling that *every* initial *en-* should be made *in-*; the change might have extended from the association group consisting of the words *en* and words of similar form and meaning to the partly identical association group consisting of words with initial *en-*. That this spread did not actually occur is shown by *enim* and *ensis* (which had short *e* at the time we are discussing), the only Latin words with initial *en-* which were not on the basis of meaning associated with either the preposition or the negative prefix.

The prerequisite for any such spread of a change from word to word is that some speakers shall feel that one sound should be substituted for another. One may get such a feeling in various ways. The people of Missouri get it when they try to substitute standard English for their native dialect, and Vespasian got it when his courtiers instructed him in standard Latin pronunciation. In both cases there is a change of models—a standard language is substituted for a local or class dialect. In other words, dialect-mixture may lead to the generalizing of a sound-change.

The same result may arise from a change in the model itself. If I admire the speech of my employer, or superior officer, or elder brother, I am likely to imitate and extend any phonetic innovation that occurs in his speech, and those who imitate my speech are likely to carry the process still farther. No records have ever been kept of these first beginnings of regular changes of sound, and so it is not possible to refer phonetic laws to their origins. We know that English *wah* has changed to *waw*, and we can give approximate dates for some stages of the process; but we do not know when or where or in whose pronunciation the first impulse toward the change occurred.

We have seen that many sound-changes are irregular when they first appear and gradually become more and more regular. The reason is that each person who substitutes the new sound for the old in his own pronunciation tends to carry it into new words. The two processes of spread from word to word and spread from speaker to speaker progress side by side until the new sound has extended to all the words of the language which contained the old sound in the same surroundings.

Isolated Changes

Many changes of form, however, spread over a language without spreading to any other words than the ones in which they originate. In some cases there is no other word with a similar combination of sounds; Latin *nutrix* from **nutritrix* could not influence other words with the sound-group *trītr* because there were none. But the spread from word to word does not always occur when it would be possible. Two chief causes for the isolation of a change of form may be mentioned.

Probably a change will not spread from a single word to other words on the basis of formal association alone. The past participle of Latin *morior* ought to be **mortus*, but the analogy of *vivus* has changed it into *mortuus;*

there surely never resulted from this change a tendency to change *t* to *tu*. The change of *h* to *f* in English "four" could not by itself cause a regular change of initial *h* to *f*. We are here forced to argue a priori, since objective data are almost wholly lacking for the reason stated on page 81; but it seems safe to say that the likelihood that a sound-change will become regular varies directly as the number and the frequency of the words which induce it.

A second cause for the isolation of a sound-change is an association of the change in question with a particular meaning. The reason why Latin *enim* did not become *inim* was that the change of initial *en-* to *in-* was felt to belong to the meanings "in-" and "un-." Analogy has appended an *s* to numerous English genitives and plurals which formerly did not have that termination; but the connection of the ending with the two meanings has been so close that there has not been the slightest tendency for this *s* to spread beyond the two categories.

It is impossible to say just how strong the association of a sound-change with a meaning must be in order to hinder its spread beyond the semantic group. Apparently the pronunciation "Missoura" is favored by association with other geographical names, such as "America," "Arizona," and "Nevada"; but the association is not strong enough to prevent the common noun "prairie" from becoming "praira."

Superficially there is a sharp contrast between regular and irregular change of form, and for the historian of language it is a distinction that must be carefully observed. Many scholars have supposed that the two were fundamentally different. It has been thought that the phonetic laws belonged solely to the physical or physiological side of language and that their regularity was as relentless as the law of gravitation—and for similar reasons—while irregular changes were psychological in their nature and were incalculable in their effects, because the mind of man is a free agent.

We have seen, however, that both kinds of sound-change are at once physiological and psychological. Indeed, the psychological factor of association is largely responsible for the regularity of many of the phonetic laws; many irregular changes of sound ultimately become regular by the operation of psychological causes. And, on the other hand, we have seen that psychological causes may hinder a change from spreading to all words which contain a given sound.

CHAPTER IV

CHANGE OF MEANING

Semantic Change Erratic

While the regular operation of the phonetic laws makes it possible to recognize a connection between widely different forms in various related languages, there is no similar clue to help us trace the changes which have affected the meanings of words. No scholar can doubt the etymological identity of Old Irish *athir* and Sanskrit *pitā*, although they have not a single sound in common; for all the differences accord with recognized phonetic laws. As wide a divergence in meaning can be traced only in case we have historic records of intermediate stages. One might well doubt the relationship of English "write" with Dutch *rijten* and German *reissen* "tear, split," if it were not for such intermediate stages as Old Saxon *wrītan* "cut" and also "write" and Icelandic *rita* "scratch, write." No one knows whether Latin *ruo* "fall" and *ruo* "rush" are related to each other or not, for we have no record of earlier stages of the Latin language which might show either greater similarity between their meanings or greater divergence.

Nevertheless we may study many changes of meaning which have taken place within the historic period, and sometimes we can reconstruct a change which occurred in prehistoric times. The branch of linguistic science which treats of the meaning of words is called **semasiology,** or **semantics,** and change in meaning is called semantic change.

85

Types of Semantic Change—Shift of Emphasis

Everyone who has used a dictionary knows that most words have several meanings; but the variation is really more extensive than a dictionary could indicate. The word "horse" in its literal meaning suggests a very large number of sensations and experiences, for each man's idea of a horse is a sort of composite photograph of the horses he has known of. But the photograph differs with every person who uses the word; for no two people have seen precisely the same horses. The farmer will see a plow horse; the drayman will see a heavy animal with hairy fetlock; the jockey will see a slender-legged, nervous thoroughbred. Then again, the word will convey a different meaning according to when and where it is used. In a zoölogical lecture a horse is an animal of a certain genus and species with a particular physiological structure. On a farm a horse is the beast that draws the plow, or it may be an animal that must be fed three times a day. At the blacksmith's a horse is an animal with four hoofs to be shod. In a treatise on meat supply in war-time, a horse is an animal whose flesh may be used instead of beef. In each case one side of the idea is emphasized at the expense of the others, and so the word has a different meaning. The hearer learns what meaning is intended, partly from the situation under which the word is spoken, and partly from the rest of the sentence and the surrounding sentences. Often a very little of the context is enough; note the varying meaning of "goes" in "the train goes," "the mill goes," "the money goes."

The emphasis on one element of a complex idea may be so strong that the other elements are forgotten.

Latin *vendito* means "offer for sale, try to sell," often by praising one's wares. So, with shift of emphasis, Cicero (*Att.* i. 16. 16) says to his friend Atticus, *valde te venditavi*, "I praised you a lot." English "knave" is the same word as German *Knabe*, and its original meaning was "boy." Many boys were servants, and emphasis on that element of the concept gave the word a new meaning; the transition stage is to be seen in *The kokes knaue, thet wassheð the disshes*[1] ("The cook's boy that washes the dishes"). Some servants are rascals, and emphasis upon that part of the idea yields the modern meaning of the word "knave." The original meaning of English "to dress" was the same as that of French *dresser* "make straight," and we still retain it in "dress ranks" and "dress timber." The latter phrase implies the cutting away of surplus material, and with emphasis on this part of the idea we get "dress hides," "dress poultry," "dress a vine." In all these phrases the verb connotes preparation, and this is the preponderant idea in "dress a salad," "dress a wound," "dress the hair." In the last phrase, and to a lesser degree in some of the others, there is an idea of adornment, which becomes emphatic in "dress a shop window" or "he dresses his wife well." The latter involves the idea of clothing, and so, finally, we get such phrases as "dress one's self." A simpler example is "end," whose first meaning is "limit," but which often means "goal," as in the phrase "an end in itself."

The circumstances under which a word is used very often lead to a change of the predominant element in its

[1] *Ancren Riwle*, (Morton), p. 380

meaning. The word "doubtless" is rarely used unless some have doubts in the matter; if a fact is really quite free from doubt one scarcely takes the trouble to say so. The word therefore comes to imply more or less doubtfulness, and sometimes this implication is the predominant part of the idea; the word "doubtless" may be employed to make a statement less positive, as "To this construction are doubtless to be referred all cases."[1]

A change in customs or environment sometimes makes a shift in emphasis inevitable. Latin *penna* meant "feather," and denoted a feather used as a writing implement as well as any other. A shift of emphasis was necessary when writing with quills became so common that this aspect of the whole idea was for many the most familiar one. The word "fee" once meant "cattle," and one element of the concept was the idea that cattle might be used to pay a debt. When cattle ceased to be used for this purpose it was no longer possible to consider payment a subordinate characteristic of cattle; it must necessarily become an independent idea. Political history is responsible for the change in meaning of Latin *praetor*. As agent noun from *prae-eo*, the word originally meant "he who goes before," and it was the title of the highest military and civil officer. By successive limitations of power, this officer's functions changed from those of general and chief magistrate to those of judge of a criminal court, and the predominant meaning of the word kept pace; hence the inconsistency in classical Latin between *praetor* "criminal judge" and *praetorium* "general's tent."

[1] Allen and Greenough, *New Latin Grammar*, p. 260.

In addition to their intellectual content words suggest certain emotions. The word "home" differs from "house" chiefly in its emotional content, and that is also the main distinction between "blockhead" and "fool," "brats" and "children," "sweetheart" and "lover." Sometimes the emphasis on the emotional content of a word becomes so great that the intellectual content is lost sight of. Many conservatives regard "anarchists" and "socialists" with equally intense dislike; and so one often hears the two words coupled, as if they applied alike to all undesirable citizens, although anarchy and socialism are really opposite extremes of political theory.

In several of the cases just discussed the shift of emphasis has led to an increase in the range of applicability of a word. The change in the meaning of "knave" from "servant boy" to "servant" was due to an exclusive emphasis on one element of the idea and the consequent elimination of the other element; and then the new meaning automatically applied to a serving man as well as to a serving boy. The decrease in the logical content of the word involved an increase in its range of applicability. Such an extension of application cannot be consciously recognized by the speaker; since "knave" means to him merely "servant," he is not aware of an innovation when he applies the word to a servant of mature years.

Worn-out Figures of Speech

The causal relation of these two processes is sometimes reversed; a word may be consciously employed in a wider application and consequently with a narrower logical content. The speaker who first called the support of a table a "leg" must have been aware that he was applying the word to a thing very different from that which it had hitherto signified; one result of the innovation was that "leg" in its new use immediately lost some of its content. Such a conscious and more or less arbitrary extension of the applicability of a word is called a figure of speech. It is often impossible to distinguish between semantic changes due to shift of emphasis and those which originate as figures of speech. A four-year-old boy saw a blanket on a horse and called it an "apron." Did he suppose that "apron" meant merely "outer covering which is not always worn," or did he mean to say, "The horse is like a woman with an apron on"? Some of the following examples possibly belong in whole or in part under the preceding topic.

Figures of speech are used for the sake of vividness, suggestiveness, and sometimes for clearness. We call a man an "ass" or we call him "sour" for emphasis and also to call up the emotions associated with the literal meanings of the words. A figurative expression contributes to clearness when a language lacks a literal word for the idea, as when we speak of a "transparent character."

When a figure is used very commonly, its figurative nature is lost, and it is understood directly in its secondary sense. Whereas the word "transparent" in the phrase "transparent character" is still a genuine figure, the word "clear" in a "clear statement" has ceased to suggest "clear water," a "clear sky," and the like, as it once did, and thereby it has suffered a change of meaning.

Faded metaphors are common in all languages. The "iris" of the eye was originally the "rainbow" of the eye. "Tulip" originally meant "turban" and was applied to the flower on account of its shape. "Daisy" is properly "day's eye" and was applied first to the sun and then by a second metaphor to the flower.

There is a strong tendency to use concrete sensuous terms for abstract suprasensuous ideas. Some purely intellectual processes are denoted by words which primarily refer to physical action. "To compose a poem" is, according to etymology, "to place it together." In the phrase "to get hold of an idea" the metaphor is still felt; but the phrase "to comprehend an idea" has in ordinary use lost entirely its metaphorical character. Other instances are "simple," which originally meant "without fold," and its derivative "simplicity"; "right," which originally meant "straight"; "hard," in such phrases as "a hard task" or "a hard character."

Terms belonging to the sphere of one sense are often made to apply to the objects of another. In "loud colors" we still feel the metaphor; "a sharp tongue" and "a high note" hardly suggest a comparison any longer.

Metonymy is the use of one word for another with which its meaning is closely connected, as when we say that one sets a "good table" and keeps a "good cellar." The fading of metonymy gives us "board," in the sense of "regular meals"; "the pulpit," meaning "the clergy"; "the bar," meaning "the lawyers"; "a chair," meaning "a professorship."

Synecdoche is the naming of a thing from one of its parts or qualities. A part is used for the whole in "hands" for "laborers," "blade" for "a sword," German *Bein* for "leg" (originally the same word as

English "bone"). Similarly, quality nouns often become collective nouns. English "youth," "the quality of being young," comes to mean "those who are young." Latin *multitudo* originally meant "the quality of being many, maniness," just as *magnitudo* means "the quality of being large, largeness," but it came to mean "that which contains many individuals, crowd." A judge is called from a characteristic "your honor"; a king, "your majesty"; a king's son, "your royal highness." Sometimes clothing gives a name, as when the clergy are called "the cloth," or when we speak of "the blue and the gray."

More Specific Meaning Due to a Modifier

Whenever one needs an expression which is more specific—that is, contains more information and applies to fewer objects—than any word in his language, he is compelled to use several words. This is the reason why we have adjectives and adverbs; there is no one word for "red book," "large apple," "six inches," "sing sweetly," and therefore we have to use phrases. Such a phrase is inconvenient and cumbersome if the idea represented is at all common, and there is a tendency to drop part of a much-used phrase, thus giving the word that is retained the more specific meaning of the phrase. Horace says *Massicum, Falernum, Caecubum* for *vinum Massicum*, etc., just as we say "Champagne," "Madeira," etc., omitting the word "wine." The word "meat" in early English meant any kind of food, and the phrase "flesh meat" was used where now we say "meat."[1]

[1] Another factor in this change may have been such phrases as "meat and bone," "meat and hide."

Latin *sermo* meant "talk"; in the Middle Ages the phrase *sermo religiosus* was very common, and now we use "sermon" in that sense without an adjective. The Latin phrase *hiberna castra* "winter camp" was simplified to *hiberna*, and thus *hiberna* changed its meaning from "of winter" to "winter camp." *Ludi* changed its meaning from "exhibitions" to "theatrical exhibitions" through the phrase *ludi scenici*. *Momentum* "movement" gets the familiar meaning "moment" from the phrase *momentum temporis*. Very striking instances of this process are the change of Latin *rem* "thing" to French *rien* "nothing" through the phrase *ne ... rien* "not a thing," and of *passum* "step" to the French negative *pas* through the phrase *ne ... pas*, which originally meant "not a step."

Many indeterminate words have thus come to suggest one of the original alternatives; English "luck" now regularly means "good luck," whereas Latin *venenum* came to mean "an ill potion, poison."

More General Meaning Due to a Pleonastic Modifier

Everybody is familiar with the attempt to make ideas clearer or more striking by expressing them twice. A preacher once announced, "An afternoon service will be substituted instead." Livy (xxi. 32. 7) says *fama prius .... praecepta res erat* "the matter had been previously anticipated by rumor." In such pleonastic phrases one word is shorn of part of its meaning. In the church notice the phrase "substituted instead" leaves only the meaning "held" for "substituted," whereas it should mean "held instead." English "with" is connected with German *wider* and originally meant "against"; but in the phrase "fight with" the idea of opposition was fully expressed in the verb, and there was nothing left to the preposition but accompaniment. The new meaning thus originated has now supplanted the old one, except in the compounds "withstand," "withdraw," "withhold." Although such changes of word-meaning are extremely rare, the process is of importance for syntax, and we shall discuss further examples under that topic.

Analogical Change of Meaning

Any change in the psychological grouping of words involves a shift of meaning. The word "shed," "a hut," is a dialectic form of the noun "shade"; but, since the word has come to be associated rather with the verb "shed" and the compound "water-shed," we think of a "shed" as a protection, not from the sun, but from the rain. The word applies to the same buildings as before, but the meaning has changed nevertheless.

The process seems at first glance to be the converse of analogical change of form, where an association of two or more words on the basis of meaning causes them to approximate one another in form. The noun "shed," on the other hand, came to be associated with the verb "shed" because of their identity of form, and the result is an approximation in meaning. As a matter of fact, however, an association close enough to produce either sort of change must be based upon a certain degree of similarity between the words affected in respect both of meaning and of form. The word *mâle* could not have changed *femelle* into "female" if the words had not already been similar in form; the noun "shed" would not have been associated with the verb "shed" if sheds had not happened to shed water. The basis of analogical change of sound and that of associative change of meaning are similar. Furthermore, the processes often go on together. There is a more definite association between English "male" and "female" than between French *mâle* and *femelle*. The colloquial Latin word from which "outrage" is derived meant merely "excess," and the large emotional content which the word now has comes from its association with the word "rage." "Shame-faced" was formerly "shamfast," formed like "stead-fast," and it meant simply "modest." The popular etymology makes the word suggest blushes and at the same time changes its form. We may therefore extend the term analogy so as to speak of analogical change of meaning.

While a false etymology may produce no change of form, it almost always alters the meaning of a word. The popular derivation of "corns" (on the feet) from "corn," "grain," instead of from Latin *cornu* "horn" has slightly modified the force of the first word. "Ears" of corn are somewhat different to our thought if we associate them with our own ears. The word "saw," "a saying," has undergone considerable change in meaning since it has been separated from the verb "say" and connected with "saw," "a cutting tool." When we say that a ship is "bound for Liverpool" the word "bound" properly means "ready to go," but association with the participle of "bind" leads us to understand it as "directed toward, compelled to go to."

Analogy may extend to an entire group of words a change of meaning which originates in a part of the group. "Execution" means "performance"; but the execution of a decree of a court may include putting a man to death, and so, with shift of emphasis, "execution" came to mean "capital punishment." Similarly, "executioner" (performer) came to mean "hangman." The verb "execute," being transitive, was held to its original meaning by the accompanying object— "he executes the decree" cannot be the source of "he executes the criminal"; but the analogy of the two words "execution" and "executioner" finally caused the verb "execute" to be used in the new sense of "put to death." Latin *valeo* meant "be well," and the second-person forms of the imperative and subjunctive, *vale, valete, valeas,* were commonly used as formulas of leave-taking. With shift of emphasis they came to mean "go away," as in the formula of divorce, *valeas, tibi habeas res tuas.* By analogy the third person got the same force. In Terence (*Andria* 889) Simo disowns his son for insisting upon a disadvantageous marriage: *immo habeat, valeat, vivat cum illa!* "he may marry her! goodby to him! let him live at her house!"

Semantic Rivalry

When a word changes in form, we expect the earlier form to be lost. There are some exceptions to this rule, as in case of an analogical change of form; or when the phonetic laws give two or more forms of a word, according to the position it occupies in the sentence; or when a word which has changed its form in a given language is later borrowed into that language, either from its own earlier literature or from a related language. In such cases, however, the two forms of the word will scarcely ever last a great while unless they are used in somewhat different senses; for example, English "skirt" and "shirt," "of" and "off," Latin *partim* "partly" beside *partem* (accusative of *pars* "part").

When a word changes in meaning, on the other hand, the old meaning is very likely to survive alongside of the new. English "youth" occurs in three meanings, which arose successively (see pages 92 and 141). Latin *miles* is much more common in its primary meaning "soldier," but is not uncommon in the secondary meaning "soldiery." English "dress" is most familiar in the sense "to clothe," but several of the more primitive meanings are still in use.

There is, nevertheless, some tendency to do away with one of two or more meanings of the same word. Sometimes the primary meaning of a word is lost, and only the secondary one preserved; Latin *multitudo* never means "numerousness," English "fee" never means "cattle."

Many have regretted the loss of old meanings and the fading of the figures of speech in which some current meanings originated. They have also urged that we could better understand the actual use of words if we were fully conscious of their history. The study of etymology, it has been supposed, is a practical help to the correct use and full understanding of a language. There is a certain aesthetic value in the knowledge that "Florida" originally meant "land of flowers," or that "daisy" is properly "the eye of day," or that "Margaret" means "pearl." But it is not often that a consciousness of a word's etymology helps to an understanding of its present meaning, and in many cases such knowledge is actually a hindrance. If a knowledge of the true etymology leads anyone to associate the noun "shed" with "shade," he will miss the present meaning of the word. Archbishop Trench, in a book that was long used as a textbook,[1] derived the word "desultory" from Latin *desultor* "one who rides two or three horses at once, leaps from one to the other, being never on the back of any one of them long." He continues: "Take, I say, the word thus to pieces, and put it together again, and what a firm and vigorous grasp will you have now of its meaning! A desultory man is one who jumps from one study to another, and never continues for any length of time in one." But when I say that Archbishop Trench's treatment of linguistic problems is desultory, I do not mean to compare the reverend gentleman with a circus rider! If the metaphors did not die out of language, the most commonplace remark would be so overloaded with impertinent suggestions that we could not discover which idea it was intended to express. Etymology is a valuable study, but we should not expect it to help us very much in understanding our mother-tongue.

[1] *The Study of Words*, p. 352.

CHAPTER V

CHANGE IN VOCABULARY

Reasons for the Loss of Words

When ideas are lost to a community, the words which denoted them drop out of use. There are many words in the English dictionary which we never have occasion to use except in speaking of the past. Since threshing machines have been introduced, we rarely speak of "flails"; and since spinning is now done by machinery, the word "distaff" is wanting in most persons' vocabularies. "Stocks," "pillory," and "whipping-post" are rare words. In another generation the schoolboy's "slate" will be as completely forgotten as his "horn-book" is now.

Unless synonyms come to be differentiated in meaning, one of them is usually lost. "Writing" and "scripture" once meant the same thing. The latter has been differentiated in meaning from the former, so that it is synonymous with "Bible," and this word has practically driven it out of use. English "yea" and "nay" were once distinguished from "yes" and "no" in that the former answered an affirmative question ("Are you going?"), while the latter answered a negative question ("Are you not going?"). When this distinction broke down, "yea" and "yes," "nay" and "no" became exact synonyms, and now "yea" and "nay" have become obsolete. In early English the principal parts of "bear" and "break" were "bear, bare, born(e)" and "break, brake, broke(n)." The analogy of such verbs as "slide, slid, slidden," "spin, spun, spun," and "fight, fought, fought," brought the vowel of the participle into the past tense and yielded the forms "bore" and "broke," which have now supplanted their older rivals.

The Polynesian word *tapu* (whence English **"taboo"**), like Latin *sacer*, must be translated into English sometimes by "sacred" and sometimes by "accursed"; the Polynesians are, as the Romans were, unconscious of the distinction, which to us seems fundamental. The Polynesian "taboo" differs from Latin *sacer* in being connected with magic rather than with religion; and yet Latin *sacer* also was largely a magician's word. A further difference is that Polynesian "taboo" applies to many more acts and objects than Latin *sacer* did. The effect of taboo is that one is forbidden to perform certain acts, to use or to touch certain objects, or to speak certain words. Commoners must not touch or speak to a king or a priest; at certain times one must not eat the flesh of certain animals; one must not enter a burying ground, except to bury the dead; brother and sister must not speak to each other or even remain in each other's presence. If asked why he is afraid to do these things the savage may reply that some harm would befall either himself or someone dear to him; the penalty may be death, disease, failure of crops, etc. In such cases the taboo is a sort of negative magic. But often no penalty can be named for the violation of a taboo; the act is not performed simply because it is regarded as improper.

If the institution of taboo were confined to Polynesia **it would not be worth our attention**; but it is found in a lesser degree in nearly all savage and semi-civilized races, and no clear distinction can be drawn between taboo and certain irrational habits of our own. Why, for example, do we not allow a railroad to condemn a right of way through a graveyard? Why do we persist in wearing clothes in the hottest summer weather? Why is it strictly forbidden to eat with one's knife?

By the vast majority of mankind names are identified with the objects for which they are used. In the Hindoo philosophic systems *nāmarūpam* "name and form" signifies "personality, the individual existence of a man"; *nāmarūpam* is even said to originate in the mother's womb. Most systems of magic take it for granted that he who knows the name of a person or object has mystic power over it. Consequently the ancient Egyptians, among others, had two personal names apiece, a "grand" name, which was carefully kept secret, and a "little" name for ordinary use. It is not strange, then, that words as well as things and acts are taboo. In various parts of the world one's own name, or the names of one's relatives, of a husband, of a wife, or of relations by marriage, must be avoided. The natives of Australia and the American Indians, among others, will not speak the name of one who is dead. The names as well as the persons of kings or chiefs are taboo. In many places words which resemble taboo names are themselves taboo. Hence when a new king ascends the throne any word which resembles his name must be given up.

Common nouns too are often taboo. Various dangerous or injurious animals may not be spoken of by their own names, because these are necessarily uncomplimentary; instead they are called "the mighty one," "the silent one," "the old man," or the like. Such circumlocutions are used for the wolf in Sweden, for the bear in Russia, for the rattlesnake by the American Indians, for the lion, the tiger, and the cobra in various tropical countries.

Very frequently the name of a god or a demon is taboo. The Furies of Greek mythology were such fearful beings that people feared they might offend them by using their proper name, Ἐρινύες; and so the Furies were called Εὐμενίδες "gracious ones." The most dreadful of the gods of the early Hindus was Rudra. According to the Brāhmanas, Prajāpati committed incest with his daughter, and the gods sought in vain for someone who should be able to punish the crime. "Then they all brought together the most fearful substances that dwelt within them into a heap: therefrom came this god," that is, Rudra; and he avenged the crime. His back is red, the color of death and everything fearful, and his belly is dark blue. It is he who sends sickness and all misfortune, his arrows are fever and cough. In the Vedas the proper name Rudra was still used freely, although the god was often addressed by such epithets as "the great god," "the ruler," "the lord of cattle," "the gracious," "the mighty," "the terrible." In later Hinduism Rudra is no longer called by his ancient name; he is now Çiva "the kind" or Nandi "the gladsome." There is no essential difference between this sort of taboo and our own avoidance of such words as "devil," "hell," "damn." Many persons prefer to say the "Almighty" instead of "God," the "Savior" instead of "Jesus" or "Christ."

In other cases our modern reticences differ considerably from taboo among savages in the meaning of the words affected, but our feeling is scarcely more rational than the old fear of naming the dead or of calling the wolf by his own name. There are many English words so strictly taboo that one dare not mention them even as examples. Very many others are avoided in polite society, for example "puke," "stink," "whore," "bastard." In fact, there seems to be a tendency to increase the scope of this sort of taboo in England and America. Some people will not use the word "belly"; there are expurgated editions of the familiar Christmas jingle which omit the lines:

> He has eyes black as ink, and a little round belly,
> That shakes when he laughs like a bowl full of jelly.

Placards were formerly posted in the Union Station at Indianapolis which read as follows: "Please do not expectorate (spit) on the platform." There are people who say "limb" for "leg," because, forsooth, women wear skirts. In England the word "bug" is taboo, because it means what we call, under our breath, "bedbug."

Reasons for the Rise of New Words

New ideas are originated with even greater frequency than old ideas are lost. In the case of new inventions, scientific discoveries, philosophical theories, etc., the new name is usually the work of one man or of a very few. Biologists are always privileged to name new species which they discover. Professor Bloomfield, of Johns Hopkins University, invented the word "haplology," which we had occasion to use above. Other recent words are "appendicitis," "motory" (motory sensations), "subliminal," "helium," "spark-plug." Hundreds of new scientific terms are originated every year. Many of them never come to be used by more than a few specialists, but some, like those just mentioned, gain a more general currency. Of course discoveries, inventions, and the origination of words to denote them are not limited to modern times. Pythagoras was unwilling to be called σοφιστής "wise man, wizard," as other thinkers of his day called themselves; and so he invented a new word, φιλόσοφος "lover of wisdom," to describe his novel attitude toward knowledge. When Cicero translated Greek philosophic writings into Latin, he was forced to invent many new words, such as *indolentia* and *qualitas* for Greek ἀπάθεια and ποιότης, respectively.

Frequently a new word springs up from the people. When the practice of putting criminals to death by means of electricity was introduced, someone invented the word "electrocute" to describe the process. Barbarously formed as the word was, its plausible resemblance to "execute" gained its immediate acceptance with the newspapers and the crowd. The introduction of the "aeroplane" brought with it that word, which is doubtless due to the inventor of the machine, and also such words as "airman," "birdman," which are already obsolete, and "aviator," which bids fair to survive.

Perhaps the most important of all new words are those which stand for new groupings of facts or new subdivisions of a class. A chief difference between the thinking of the savage and that of the civilized man is that the former tends to perceive objects separately, often taking note of comparatively minute differences between them, but more rarely grouping them into classes, while civilized man tends to notice resemblances and to form classes. In other words, civilized thinking is increasingly conceptual. Languages reflect this psychological difference. The Bakaïri Indians of South America have names for several varieties of parrots, but no word for "parrot"; they distinguish many kinds of palm trees, but have no word for "palm-tree" in general. The primitive Indo-European language had a word for "father" and one for "mother," but there is no evidence that it had a word for "parent"; there was an astonishing number of words to designate relatives of various degrees, but, so far as the evidence goes, no word for "relative" in general. There are savage tongues which use distinct words to indicate how many objects are meant; one word, for example, will denote "one coconut," and quite a different one, "three coconuts." In the personal pronouns of the Indo-European languages we have a trace of this state of affairs. Even in English the first personal pronoun consists of four distinct words, "I," "me," "we," "us."

All languages, especially those of civilized races, are frequently enriched by the introduction of new general terms. The Dutch chemist Van Helmont conceived the idea of a category which should include all such substances, as "air," "oxygen," "hydrogen," etc., and called it "gas." Most names of scientific genera are general terms of recent invention, as are also such comprehensive terms as "vertebrate" and "invertebrate." In this field, however, language lags behind the intellectual life of a people; a new class-name cannot appear until a concept has been formed which it is to represent, but the word need not at once follow the rise of the concept. We often think of "knife," "fork," and "spoon" as the utensils with which we eat, and in Italian the three together are called *posate;* in standard English the concept lacks a name, although housewives sometimes use the phrase "flat silver" in this sense. There is no one word for the articles sold in a bookstore, namely, books, periodicals, and stationery. Neither is there a name for substances that float in water. I once lived at a small boarding-house for students where breakfast was likely to be a hurried meal. When a boarder appeared in the dining-room, the waiter brought him a dish of cereal and a cup of coffee. Then arose a need for sugar, milk, and spoon, and the only way to get them was to ask another boarder to pass them; it seemed greedy to ask for the three in one breath, and yet if you asked for only one you would ordinarily get only that. We all longed in vain for a general term to include the three until a brilliant Freshman called them the "fixings."

While some savages are content with specific names for objects which interest them—names which designate each minute species and leave the genus undesignated—they have for objects which do not arouse so much interest only vague general terms without any designation for the particulars. The Bakaïri Indians have one word which means "thunder" and "lightning" and another for "rain," "thunderstorm," and "cloud." That is, they can speak of a cloud only by calling it "rain," and the most violent thunderstorm comes under the same term. The difference of this from a group-name, such as English "storm," is apparent. A child speaks in the manner of a savage when he calls all men "papa," all liquids "water," all animals by the first animal name he happens to learn.

Advancing civilization frequently invents specific names for details not hitherto named. English has always had a word for "cloud," although Anglo-Saxon *wolken* was in no way related to the modern term. The names of the different kinds of cloud, however—"cirrus," "cumulus," "nimbus," etc.—are comparatively new. Ancient languages, even Latin and Greek, were poor in color-words and inexact in the use of those that they had. Modern speech is enriched every few years by the introduction of a new color-name of quite exact meaning.[1]

Many new words are due to a desire for novelty. Such are the slang words which spring suddenly into popularity and for a few months seem amusing enough to enliven the dullest conversation, but which presently send a shudder down the spine of one whose slang is up to date. Not long since I heard a professor of my acquaintance remark jauntily, "You're off your base." That phrase was once as fresh and spicy as "have a heart" or "do one's bit" is now; but to use such anti-quated slang today is equivalent to labeling yourself a has-been. Who wants to call his partner in the Platts-burg military trot a "lulu" or the music "hot stuff"? Yet that is what one said in the days before the schot-tische went out of vogue! George Ade's Artie called

---

[1] No doubt the development of new dyestuffs has a great deal to do with new color-names; but the colors all exist in nature and might have been named a thousand years ago if men's attention had been drawn to them.

dollars "cases" or "simoleons." About the year 1910 the word "skiddoo" was a favorite imperative for contemptuous dismissal.

Occasionally a word introduced for the sake of novelty finds a permanent place in the language. "Mob" was originally a jesting abbreviation of the phrase *mobile vulgus*, and for many years it was regarded as slang. English "gamin" comes from the French, where it was originally slang. There is some indication that the slang word "eats" for "refreshments" will make a place for itself.

When religious feeling, modesty, or prudery leads to the loss of a word, its place is sometimes supplied by an old word or phrase used in a new sense. Many persons say "hades" for "hell," "stomach" for "belly," "perfume" for any kind of a smell. A phrase may be substituted for a tabooed word. Shakespeare's thieves call themselves "St. Nicholas' clerks" or "minions of the moon." A small boy who had been taught not to say "devil" was asked what the day's sermon was about and replied, "About the gentleman that keeps hell."

In other cases the taboo leads to the use of a new word. We say "vomit" instead of "puke," "procurer" for "pimp" or "pander," "perspiration" for "sweat." A few persons say "expectorate" instead of "spit." "Palm-oil" takes the place of "bribe" with practical politicians. "Head-money" is a bribe paid for a vote. "Love-child" is used to avoid the odium of "bastard." Of course there is no end to the invention of new names for unpleasant things; each of them presently becomes contaminated and has to be abandoned in its turn. To the Greeks the left side was unlucky, and since it was a bad omen to mention ill fortune they avoided the word for "left." Hence λαιός and σκαιός (cognate with Latin *laevus* and *scaevus*) gave way to ἀριστερός, "the better," and when this too became a word of ill omen people substituted εὐώνυμος, "of good name."

A change of models may lead to the introduction of new words. Some American imitators of the English like to say "shop" instead of "store," "chemist" instead of "druggist," "tram" instead of "street car." Many speakers of English and German like to employ French words, particularly for anything that has to do with eating or getting married. Hence we have "chef" and "fiancée," "table d'hôte" and "trousseau," "café noir," and "divorcée."

Sources of New Words—Analogical Creation

By far the most important means of enriching the vocabulary is analogical creation, a subject to which we have alluded (pages 42 f.), but which demands further treatment here. In standard English we have the words "enthusiasm," "enthusiast," and "enthusiastic," but since there is no corresponding verb we are compelled to use the cumbrous phrases "to become enthusiastic" and "to make enthusiastic." Aside from their excessive length these locutions are unsatisfactory because they differ from the other members of the group more widely than is justified by a difference in function. To meet this want the verb "enthuse" has been formed. It has not yet won its way into good usage, but it fills a real need and will probably become a permanent part of the language.

As we observed before, the tendency toward analogical creation can always be represented in the form of a problem in proportion.   The German personal pronouns have separate forms for accusative and dative singular, *mich, mir; dich, dir;* but the reflexive has only one form for the two cases.   Some dialects have formed a new dative, as a result of the tendency which we may formulate, *dich*:*dir*=*sich*:*x* (*sir*).   Ordinarily the formula is not so simple as this, unless we arbitrarily abbreviate it. Vulgar English has formed the verbs "elocute" and "evolute" after the nouns "elocution" and "evolution." The pairs of words which led to the new formations were extremely numerous; a partial statement of the formula is "construct":"construction"="subtract":"subtraction"="promote":"promotion"="regulate":"regulation"="emulate" : "emulation"="constitute" : "constitution"="execute" : "execution"=*x* : "elocution"= *x*:"evolution."   In such a case it is usual to select one or two pairs to represent the entire group and to state the problem and its solution together: "execute":"execution"="evolute":"evolution."

Composition

A phrase which has been fused into a single word is called a compound word.   The change from phrase to word is gradual, and many expressions may be considered either as phrases or as compound words.   Is "apple-pie" one word or two? Is "nevertheless" one word or three? If it is one word, what shall we say of the equivalent expression, "for all that"? There is the same question about the Latin *quemadmodum*, and *senatusconsultum;* about the German *möglicherweise*

and *wenngleich*. In general we may say that we are
dealing with a compound word and no longer with a
phrase when the whole is in any way isolated so as to
be felt as a unit. Latin *denuo* from *dénovo* is isolated
by the change of *ov* to *u* in the unaccented syllable.
English "anew" was originally "of new," for we habitually say "a" for "of" before a consonant ("a matter a
fact," "a pound a tea"). "Anew," however, is no
longer felt as a phrase, because "new" without the
article is no longer used as a substantive. "Mid-
night" and "midday" are felt as compounds, because
their first element is a word no longer used in ordinary
speech. "Railroad" is isolated by the fact that it does
not apply to all roads made of rails (not, for example,
to roads made of wooden rails lying crosswise), and it
is still further isolated by the information it conveys,
which cannot be inferred from the syntactic combination
of its elements; for "railroad" means, in part, "a road
constructed of steel rails laid upon wooden crossties
for the rapid passage of heavy cars propelled by steam
or electricity." Other compounds which are isolated
by the large amount of meaning packed into them are
English "typewriter," "fireworks," German *Fern-
sprecher* "telephone," Latin *verisimilis*, which is not
merely "like the truth," but also "probably true,
probable," Greek Διόσκουροι, which designates two
particular sons of Zeus, namely, the twins Castor and
Pollux.

Not all compounds, however, can be explained as
stereotyped phrases. When compounds of a given
type have become familiar in a language, new compounds
of similar form and meaning are made by analogical

creation. At the time when illuminating gas was introduced English had long possessed the compounds "sunlight," "daylight," "firelight," "candlelight," "lamplight." Since that day the group has been extended by the analogical compound "gaslight." Many German compounds, such as *Glücksrad* and *Tageslicht*, have a genitive as prior member. On the analogy of these have been formed many compounds, like *Bildungskraft*, with feminines in the prior member, although feminines never have a genitival *s* when they stand in ordinary syntactic relations. The formula is *Glück*: *Glücksrad* = *Bildung*: *Bildungskraft*.

A similar explanation must be sought for the stem-compounds of the inflected Indo-European languages. Latin *armiger*, *multiplex*, *triangulus*, Greek ἱππόδαμος "horse-taming," δημοκρατία "democracy," ἀριστοκρατία "aristocracy," Sanskrit *indra-guptas* "protected by Indra," and many others have forms as prior members which have no independent existence. It is commonly supposed that this type of compound arose in very early times when noun-stems were used as words, that is, before the inflection of the noun was fully developed. Some compounds formed then survived the completion of the noun-declension, and these served as models for the creation of other compounds. Assuming that Latin *letifer* was one of the type-words, we may account for the formation of *fatifer* by the formula, *letum fero*: *letifer* = *fatum fero*: *fatifer*. It has recently been suggested that the type-words for these formations were not properly compounds at all, but simple words which came to be analyzed into two parts. Whether this theory is true or not, Latin *fatifer* and the great mass of similar words are certainly compounds formed after pre-existing types precisely as English "gaslight" was formed.

Derivation

A majority of all new words are formed from old words by the processes of derivation. From the point of view of grammar there are four of these: derivation by suffix, derivation by prefix, significant change in the body of a word, and inverse derivation. All are cases of analogical creation.

We usually think of a **suffix** as an independent linguistic element which may be mechanically added to words or stems. Tennis players have introduced the noun "server," which seems to consist of the verb "serve" plus the suffix -*er*. This simple and obvious explanation of derivatives is the one implied by all our grammatical terminology. The fallacy in it is the assumption that a suffix is separable from the stem, in other words, that -*er* by itself indicates the agent. The problem in the minds of those who originated the noun "server" was not, "What shall we add to the verb 'serve' to name the man who serves?" but, "What is the word that stands to 'serve' as 'player' stands to 'play'?" We do not mean to imply that any problem was consciously proposed; the need of a word and familiarity with the pair "play":"player" and many similar pairs produced the new term without conscious reflection. When the verb "pump" was formed from the noun "pump," it was furnished with an inflection by a series of analogical creations: "help" : "helps"="pump" : "pumps"; "help" : "helped"="pump" : "pumped"; "help": "helping"="pump":"pumping." The term suffix is useful as a label for certain bits of speech material, but a suffix can be transferred from word to word only by analogy.

Many suffixes originate in compound words. We have seen that a phrase is fused into a compound word by the gradual obscuring of its parts. The process does not always cease with the isolation of the word; we are fully conscious of the etymology of "bodyguard," but in "breakfast" the obscuration has gone so far that the naïve speaker never thinks of the etymological meaning, although most persons know it. Many compounds contain a member that is no longer recognizable; in "bishopric," "cowslip," and "bridal" we are aware of the first element, but not of the second. In such cases as these analogical creation may make a suffix out of the obscured member of the compound. Aside from such Old English compounds as "shameful," "sorrowful," "thankful," "baleful," we have a number of newly formed derivatives, such as "respectful," "forgetful," "masterful," which were never felt as compounds. They are due to such proportions as: "shame":"shameful" = "respect":"respectful."

There are three conditions which must usually be present before compounds can yield suffixes in this way: (1) The prior members of the compounds must keep their identity, for otherwise the proportion will lack its first extreme. (2) The final member must have the same meaning in several compounds, or else it must appear in one compound which is common enough and important enough to establish the type. (3) The meaning of the final member must be general enough so that it can be used in other words. All three of these conditions were present in the compound "shameful." "Bishopric" has not yielded a suffix because the element -*ric* does not occur in other words. "Cowslip" lacks both the second and the third condition.

Another suffix abstracted from compounds is probably to be seen in the Latin adverbs *acriter, ferociter*, etc. *Breviter* seems to have been originally a phrase, *breve iter* "by the short road." In course of time the phrase became a compound *breviter*, like German *kurzweg* and English "straightway." There must have been other compounds containing the same final element; perhaps *celeriter* was one of them; but most of the adverbs in -*ter* are based on adjectives which can scarcely have modified the noun *iter*. After the origin of the final member had been forgotten, it was transferred as a suffix on the basis of such proportions as *brevis* (genitive) : *breviter* = *acris* : *acriter*.[1] The French future suffix originated in the same way. *Donnerai, finirai* were originally compounds of infinitives with the verb-form *ai* "have." Present-day speakers, however, do not feel the words as compounds, but as derivatives with a suffix -*rai*.

Analogical creation sometimes makes a suffix out of a variation which has arisen through the action of phonetic laws or in some other way. The distinction

[1] *Audacter, prudenter*, etc., may have been shortened by syncope, or they may have originated from the relation of the nominative to the adverb; *brevis* : *breviter* = *audax* : *audacter*. *Duriter* is for *durum iter*, and *aliter* may be **aliiter* with dissimilative loss. Delbrück (*Grundriss*, III, 631) thinks that the adverbs in -*ter* were formed on the model of *inter, praeter, circiter*, etc., but I can find no formula to explain the creation of *aliter* on the model of *circiter*. No doubt the two groups of adverbs reinforced each other, but in origin they must be kept apart.

between "my" and "mine," "thy" and "thine" was
originally phonetic, like that between "a" and "an."
In course of time "my" and "thy" came to be used
where the noun was expressed after them, "mine" and
"thine," where it did not follow. By analogical creation
we get the vulgar pronouns "hisn," "hern," "yourn,"
"theirn," where *n* is a suffix. In such German plurals
as *Ochsen* and *Rinder* the syllables -*en* and -*er*, respectively, were originally parts of the stem (corresponding
to *in* and *er* in Latin *homines* and *genera*). At first *n*
and *r* occurred in certain cases of the singular, as in
Latin, but in course of time the shorter stem-forms (corresponding in a way to *homo* and *genus*) came to be used
in all cases of the singular, the forms with *n* and *r* in the
plural. At this point analogical creation introduced
the plurals *Hirten, Soldaten, Thaten, Wörter, Bücher*, etc.,
beside singulars which never had an *n* or *r*.

It is sometimes said that foreign suffixes are borrowed.
This is actually done sometimes by way of jest, as when
Cicero uses the Greek suffix-τεον to make from Latin
facio a form *facteon*. The sentence runs as follows:
"Quare, ut opinor, φιλοσοφητέον, id quod tu facis, et
istos consulatus non flocci *facteon*." I have heard the
German participial prefix *ge-* used with English verbs
in a similar spirit; for example, "I have not *ge-went*."
Aside from such quips, prefixes and suffixes are not
borrowed; only complete words are taken over from one
language into another.

Sometimes, however, a foreign suffix is naturalized
by analogical creation. If a language borrows from
another a number of primitive words and a derivative
from each with the same suffix, that suffix may form new

derivatives in the borrowing language. We have borrowed from the French a great many such pairs as "degrade":"degradation," "form":"formation," "note": "notation," and on the basis of these we have formed new derivatives from English verbs, for example, "starvation" from "starve," "flirtation" from "flirt"; the suffix is even found in some peculiarly colloquial words, such as "botheration," "murderation," "thunderation."

A very interesting group of suffixes is the one seen in "baptize," "baptist," and "baptism." These three words are Greek βαπτίζω, βαπτιστής, βαπτισμός, the first of which is derived from βάπτω "dip," while the others are derived from βαπτίζω. All three were taken into Latin by the early Christians and reached English by way of the French. A number of other words with the same suffixes have reached the modern world by the same route, for example, "syllogize" and "syllogism," "evangelize" and "evangelist." These suffixes have all been naturalized in French, and many new groups have originated there, as *réaliser, réaliste, réalisme.* The suffix *-iste* in particular is as familiar as anything in the language. When, in September, 1914, General Gallieni promised the people of Paris to defend them *jusqu'au bout*, the phrase was adopted as a watchword of the patriotic cause, and presently the patriots called themselves *jusqu'au boutistes*. English has borrowed many groups of these French formations, for example, "realize," "realist," "realism," and today there are scarcely any English suffixes that are used with greater freedom than these three; every newspaper contains such recent coinages as "revolutionize," "bossism," "pacifist," "pacifism." The last two examples are interesting because they illustrate the falsity of the opinion that suffixes are mechanically appended to words or stems; there is no such word or stem as *pacif*. These words originated in a psychological process which we may represent by the formula, "economic" : "economist"= "pacific" : "pacifist" (cf. A. H. Weston, *New York Nation*, CV [1917], 174 f.).

Prefixes are transferred from word to word in the same way as suffixes; the new word "unequal" was formed from the loan-word "equal" on the model of such pairs as "like":"unlike."

If an identical prior member of a number of compounds becomes obscure, while the various final members retain the meanings which they have as separate words, the result may be a prefix. Latin *minus* in the sense of "not" entered into a number of compounds as prior member, and thus yielded the French prefix *mé-*, *més-*, which appears in *mésaventure*, *mésalliance*, *mécreant*. When these and similar words were taken over into English, their initial syllable was connected by false etymology with the prefix of English "misdeed," etc., and hence the Old French *més-* was changed to the *mis-* of English "misadventure," "misalliance," "miscreant," etc. The Modern English prefix *mis-* is in part of native origin and in part due to these French loan-words. Our prefix *re-* comes altogether from such pairs of French loan-words as "form":"reform," "generate":"regenerate," and "iteration":"reiteration."

The **variation in the body of the words** between English "drive" and "drove" was not originally significant. The vowels correspond historically to those of the cognate Gothic *dreiba* "I drive" and *draib* "I drove," and the same variation appears in Greek λείπω "leave," perfect λέλοιπα. The alternation originated in some unknown way in the Indo-European parent-language. In all the historic idioms which retain it, except some of the Germanic languages, it is accompanied by other variations in prefix or suffix, or both, which really carry the temporal force. Even in Gothic, in Anglo-Saxon, and to a certain extent in Modern German present and preterite are distinguished by different systems of personal endings as well as by the vowel of the base. In Modern English, however, barring the third person ˌsingular, the only difference between "drive" and "drove," "sing" and "sang," "bear and "bore" is the difference in vowel; a change in vowel alone is enough to alter the tense. On the model of these and other inherited pairs new preterites have been formed as follows: "drive":"drove"="strive": "strove" (a French word), "sing":"sang"="ring": "rang" (Anglo-Saxon *hringde*), "bear":"bore"= "wear":"wore" (Anglo-Saxon *werode*).

We have seen that the different vocalism of English "man" and "men," "foot" and "feet," etc., arose by assimilation of *a* to the *i* of the old plural suffix *-iz* (**manniz* became **menniz* and this became "men"). Here again the change in vowel was not significant until the ending was lost.

The process of derivation by change within the body of the word is carried very far by the Semitic languages, whose vocabulary is built up in large part from a number of roots consisting of three consonants each. Various modifications of the basic idea are marked by the insertion of different vowels and consonants between the radical consonants. The Semitic languages exhibit these triliteral roots in their earliest records (far more ancient than the earliest remains of Indo-European speech), and, since the same system is to be observed in the related language of the ancient Egyptians, we must push the origin of this method of derivation back to a time many centuries earlier than our earliest records of either Semitic or Egyptian. Nevertheless it is probable that the triliteral system arose in some such way as the English inflections "drive":"drove," "man":"men," etc.

When the pair "execute":"execution" calls up a new word "evolute" to correspond to "evolution," the new form is in reality a derivative. It differs, however, in several respects from most derivatives. Instead of being longer than the word from which it is derived, it is actually shorter; it lacks a suffix which "evolution" contains. Moreover, it is created as a parallel to words, like "execute" which are the primitives from which "execution," etc., are derived; and accordingly "evolute" is felt by most of those who use it to be the word from which "evolution" is derived.

This does not differ psychologically from other kinds of derivation, but its results are so different that we are justified in calling it **inverse derivation.** It is less common than derivation by suffix or prefix, but examples are to be found in all languages. Latin *pugnare* is a derivative of *pugnus* "fist," and *pugna* is an inverse derivative from the verb on the basis of such pairs as *fuga:fugare*. Latin *undare* "surge" is a derivative of *unda* "wave." With the verbal prefix *ab-* we have *abundare* "overflow," and from this comes the inverse derivative *abunde* "abundantly," which is formed on the model of *firmare*:*firme*, etc.

Variant Forms

Phonetic laws and analogical change may produce two words from one. In early Latin a short final vowel was omitted in rapid speech before an initial consonant of the following word, yielding the variants *neque* and *nec, face* and *fac, deinde* and *dein*. Analogy changed *honos* to *honor*, and the old form survived alongside the new. While such doublets do not arise on account of any need in the language, they may supply an additional word, a need for which happens to exist. Examples of the differentiation in the meaning of doublets are "shoal" and "shallow," "of" and "off," "not" and "naught," "shade" and "shadow." In the earliest Latin *deivos* was used as a noun meaning "god" and as an adjective meaning "divine." Phonetic law changed the nominative into *deus* and the genitive into *divi*. Analogy filled out a declension for each of the two, and then *deus* was specialized as a noun, while *divus* retained the original freedom of use in both functions. A trace of the adjectival use of *deus* is probably to be seen in the phrase *Dis Manibus* "to the Divine Manes" frequently inscribed on tombs.

Loan-Words

The English vocabulary has been enormously enlarged by loans from foreign languages. In the period from the eighth to the tenth centuries a great many Scandinavian words were adopted. For some centuries after the Norman conquest vast numbers of French words were naturalized. Ever since England became a maritime nation, and particularly since the establishment of English-speaking nations in distant parts of the world, words have been freely adopted from nearly all known tongues. America's contributions include "wigwam," "wampum," and "tomahawk" from the Indian languages; "adobe," "corral," and "ranch" from the Spanish of the southwest; "sauerkraut," "smear-case," and "wiener-wurst," or "wienies," from the German colonies in the large cities. Asia is represented, for example, by Chinese "tea," Japanese "kimono," Malay "gong," Hindoo "jungle," Persian "pagoda," Arabic "sherbet." Australia gives us "kangaroo" and "boomerang." From Africa come "chimpanzee," "gorilla," "gnu," "zebra." Most words introduced by translators and by scholars in general come from written language. They are sometimes taken from modern literatures (German "ablaut" and "umlaut"), but more commonly from the classical languages (Greek "drama," "cosmos," "chaos"; Latin "ictus," "adjective," "adverb").

Languages differ enormously in the number of foreign words they have borrowed. To change classical Sanskrit into certain of the later Hindoo languages one need do little else than apply certain sound-changes and allow for a few analogical changes in declension and conjugation. The translation of Anglo-Saxon into Modern English, on the other hand, consists very largely in substituting loan-words for Teutonic words that have gone out of use. English, in fact, contains more borrowed words than any other of the cultivated languages of Europe; but it still retains so much native material that there is no difficulty in classifying it as a Germanic language. Albanian, although on the basis of its structure and some of its most common words it is called an independent branch of the Indo-European family, has borrowed so much Latin that it has to be included in comparative grammars of the Romance languages.

Instead of borrowing a foreign word, one may combine native linguistic elements on the foreign model. Oertel cites the words "overdrive" and "overdriven" from a writer who clearly had in mind German *übertreiben* and *übertrieben*. "Aeroplane" is giving way to "airplane." The efforts made in Germany in the last fifty years or so to "purify" the language of foreign elements have, for example, substituted *Kurzschrift* for *Stenographie*, *Eindecker* for *Monoplan*, *Vertrag* for *Kontrakt*. This selfconscious modern reform is at bottom in harmony with a tendency that has long existed; Goethe substituted *Wasserleitung* for *Aquaeduct*, *umlaufen* for *circulieren*, *Zwischenreich* for *Interregnum*.[1]

The translators of the Bible are anxious to represent the exact force of the original and also to be understood. Loan-words would be quite exact, but only native speech material can be understood. Hence the Vulgate represents Greek συμπαθέω by *compatior*, ὑπερεκπερισσοῦ by *superabundanter*, συνοικέω by *cohabito*, συναιχμάλωτος by *concaptivus*. Christianity was carried to the Germans by the Roman church, and therefore Latin words rather than Greek are reflected in the German technical terms of Christianity. *Compatior*, itself an example of this process, has yielded *mitleiden*, *compater* gives *Gevatter*,

[1] For other German examples, see F. W. G. Heuser, *Germanistic Society Quarterly*, IV, 26–46.

conscientia is reflected by *Gewissen*. Cicero resorted to the same device in translating Greek philosophy, as when he coined *indolentia* on the model of Greek ἀπάθεια.

A very important group of borrowed words consists of proper names, as when a man is spoken of in a language not his own; "Cicero" is a word which all civilized languages have borrowed from the Latin. There are a few exceptions to the rule, as when a Chinaman in the United States is known to his neighbors as the "Chink" or "John," or a German is known as the "Dutchman." A few persons, on moving to a new country, translate their names or arbitrarily change them; some of the American "Smiths" were called *Ferreiro*, *Ferrajo*, or *Schmidt* in the old country, and a few of our new fellow-citizens have assumed the surname "American." Still it is generally true that a personal name is transferred from one language to another with only such phonetic alteration as all loan-words are subject to.

Names of tribes, races, and countries are usually borrowed from the language of the people concerned. Here again there are a few exceptions. The Spanish discoverers of America gave the "Indians" an Asiatic name. The first Teutonic invaders of England called the natives *welisce men* "foreigners," and we still call them "Welshmen." Cities also usually have the same name the world over, although there are instances of the change of a city-name, as when Constantine renamed "Byzantium" in his own honor, or when "New Amsterdam" fell into the hands of the British and became "New York." Rivers, mountains, etc., are likely to have the same name in all languages, and they usually keep their name whatever language comes to be spoken in their neighborhood. Most American rivers have Indian names, such as "Connecticut," "Mississippi," "Illinois"; but, oddly enough, mountains in the United States usually have English names.

Words from Proper Names

The tendency of proper names to remain the same in spite of a change from one language to another is one side of the general isolation of proper names from other speech material. Even the phonetic laws often leave proper names untouched; gradual changes, such as that of Latin unaccented $\breve{a}$ to $\breve{i}$, probably always affect them, but a sound-change that spreads from word to word may or may not be applied by any individual to his own name, and we usually pronounce a man's name according to his preference.

The isolation of proper names is not complete, however. They may spring from other linguistic material, as Miller, Stephenson, Cascade City, Bald Mountain, Little River. Conversely proper names frequently yield other proper names, common nouns, and even verbs.

Geographical names are often based upon personal names, especially in the newly discovered parts of the world, for example, Peary Land, Grinnell Land, and Smith Sound in the Arctic region. Numerous American towns have taken their names from persons. Sometimes the personal name is in the genitive case followed by a common noun, as in Wale's Station, Stewartstown, Huntsville, Williamsburg. Sometimes the personal name becomes an adjective, as in Mason City, or the prior element of a compound, as in Reedtown and Jacksonville. Any of these names may lose one of its elements in familiar speech. Mechanicsburg, Indiana, is known in its neighborhood as "the Burg," and Elkhorn, Missouri, as "the Horn." More frequently the generic word is lost and the distinctive part of the name is kept. Thus Marshalltown is spoken of as "Marshall," and Pike's Crossing as "Pike's," while Boise City has determined to put away crude things by dropping the "City." (Has Idaho heard of New York City?) Since "Pike's," "Goodall's," "Lovett's," etc., are obviously genitives, there is a tendency to form new nominatives, "Pike," "Goodall," "Lovett." Probably place-names which had gone through the process illustrated by "Marshall" for Marshalltown or the one illustrated by "Pike" for Pike's Crossing furnished the first models for the naming of towns from personal names without change or addition, for example, Jackson, Harper, Pierce, Madison.

Rivers and mountains furnish names for towns. Towns give names to railways, roads, and all sorts of institutions, among others, colleges. The Chicago River has named the city; the city has named the Chicago & Alton Railroad, the Chicago Athletic Club, the Chicago Opera House, the University of Chicago, and consequently, the Chicago football team, the Chicago colors, etc.

More important is the use of proper names or their derivatives as common nouns or verbs. We call a rich man a "Croesus," an old man a "Methuselah"; Shylock calls Portia "a Daniel come to judgment." The Assyrians have been named the "Romans of Asia." Nearly every American college town in the West or in the South boasts of being the "Athens of the West." A mountainous region in North Carolina is known in the

guide books as the "Switzerland of America"; so also
Yosemite, Lake George, Lake Louise in the Canadian
Rockies. Any of these metaphors might become stereotyped in the manner already indicated; and, as a matter
of fact, the name "Caesar" has become a common noun
in German *Kaiser* and Russian *Tsar*. Men's discoveries
and inventions are often named after them; for example,
"Bright's disease," the "Pasteur filter," the "Morse
telegraph," the "Morse code." By the loss of the
generic term we get such an expression as, "The opera-
tor's *Morse* was excellent." Other circumstances, too,
may attach a man's name to a thing or an act. "To
burke one" is to smother him and sell his body for dissec-
tion, as a certain Burke of Edinburgh did. The "boy-
cott" is named from the first prominent victim of the
system.

Derivatives of proper names are common; for
example, "pasteurize," "the Caesarian operation."
While Porfirio Diaz was dictator of Mexico, a certain
politician was accused of attempting to "diazify" the
United States. History is full of such terms as
"Medize," "the Sullan revolution," "the Napoleonic
wars." No speaker is ordinarily conscious that "peach"
is properly "Persian < apple > "and "damson," " < plum
from > Damascus."

Original Creation

So far we have been discussing the formation of new
words from speech material already in existence. A
really new creation of linguistic material is so rare that
it should be assumed only on the strongest evidence;
nevertheless it does occur.

Some of the most familiar cases of original creation result from what the psychologists call expression movements. "Every mental process has some way of expressing itself through the body; or, in other words, there is always some bodily sign which tells us, if we are good observers, that a certain mental process is in our neighbor's consciousness."[1] These bodily signs of mental processes are most pronounced in the case of emotions. Darwin describes the marks of fear as follows:

> That the skin is much affected under the sense of great fear, we see in the marvelous and inexplicable manner in which perspiration immediately exudes from it. This exudation is all the more remarkable as the surface is then cold. . . . . The hairs also on the skin stand erect; and the superficial muscles shiver. . . . . The salivary glands act imperfectly; the mouth becomes dry, and is often opened and shut.[2]

Darwin refers to the effect which fear has upon the muscles of the mouth and throat; other emotions also affect the organs of speech, and the result is frequently a sound; hence the cries of young children and of the deaf. A sound which in the first instance was due to an expression movement may be repeated or may be imitated by others to suggest the circumstances under which the sound was first made. In this way we get some of our conventional interjections. "Oo" is often heard as an expression for pleasant sensation, but seems not to have got into the dictionaries. "Oh" as an interjection for surprise and "ow" and "ouch" for sudden pain have long had lexical treatment; so has the grunt of disgust ("ugh") and the

[1] Titchener, *Primer of Psychology*, p. 62.

[2] *The Expression of the Emotions in Man and Animals*, p. 290 (Appleton, 1888).

grunt of disdain ("humph"). Such interjections as these are even more distinct from the general body of speech than are proper names; but still ordinary words may be made from them. German *ächsen* is a derivative of *ach*. Greek ἀλαλάζειν is from ἀλαλαί, and ἐλελίζειν is from ἐλελεῦ.

The various cries which we use to attract attention, such as "boo" and "hello" and "hey," are perhaps not due to expression movements, but they seem to be original creations of a similar nature. "Hem" was in the first instance the sound made by clearing the throat in preparation for speaking, and hence it came to have value for attracting attention. The word may also be used as a verb, "He hemmed and hawed." The interjections *sh*, *ss*, and *st* have given rise to the words "hush," "hiss," and "hist," the first two of which have derivatives, "hushed," "husher," "hisses," "hissing," etc.

As one watches an exciting game or any other effort which arouses sympathy, one has an impulse to imitate the movements observed. I have seen an umpire at basket-ball attract the attention of an entire audience by the ludicrous way in which he played the game on the sidelines. Singers say that after hearing very high notes they find that they have strained their vocal chords and become hoarse. It is not incredible, then, that the sight of a swaying object should set the lips to swinging and lead to the utterance of a sound like German *bammeln* "sway," which some suppose to have originated in this way.[1]

[1] I am aware that the example is not perfect, since *bammeln* is probably connected in some way with *Baum;* but it must be used until a better one is suggested, for the probability that words have been formed in about this way is very great.

Somewhat similar to this, but involving more or less conscious effort, is the imitation of a sound in nature. There are very many words which seem to mimic the sounds they signify; "thunder," "grumble," "ring," and all such words are sometimes called onomatopoetic. In many cases, however, this imitative character did not originally belong to them. When our word "thunder" is traced back to the Anglo-Saxon, it loses a considerable part of its sonorousness, and the corresponding verb *þunian* roars even more gently. The related verbs, Latin *tonet* and Sanskrit *tanvati*, do not suggest thunder at all. Furthermore, the root of all these words, *ten*, seems to be a by-form of the root *sten* which appears in Greek στένειν "to groan" and στόνος "a groan." It is then by no means certain that the original meaning was "thunder," and it is exceedingly improbable that the word was originally an imitation of thunder. Some words, however, are clearly imitative. A number of interjections are mere echoes of sounds, for example, "kerplunk," "biff," "bing," German *bums*.

The names of birds are very often imitations of their cries. In English we have "chewink," "bobolink," "chickadee," "chough," "curlew," "dickcissel," "pewee." The names "bobwhite" and "whippoor-will" owe their present form to contamination with older linguistic material.

CHAPTER VI

CHANGE IN SYNTAX

Up to this point we have confined our attention chiefly to the smaller linguistic elements—words, syllables, and sounds. The processes which we have been considering, however, affect phrases and sentences, and in some respects their operation upon these larger speech-units differs from anything we have yet observed. The name syntax forms a convenient label for that treatment of linguistic problems which does not arbitrarily confine its attention to single words; but it will be evident in what follows that there is no clear line of division between syntax and other parts of grammatical science.

Analogy

In sentence structure even more than in other aspects of language, analogy is a factor of prime importance. While a speaker can learn a large vocabulary by rote and draw on his memory for each word he wants to use, such a treatment of sentences is quite impossible. Many sentences, to be sure, may be and regularly are exactly reproduced from memory, for example, "Here I am," "Where is it?" "Good morning," "It's a warm day"; but even the least talkative of men speaks far more sentences than he could commit to memory. Most of them are built up by analogical creation; remembering the type sentence "It's a warm day," the speaker makes a new sentence "It's a warm

summer." The formula is "day": "It's a warm day"=
"summer": "It's a warm summer." Since analogy
is constantly employed in forming our sentences it is
particularly easy for analogy to effect a change in syntax.

The cardinal numerals are very closely associated
with one another on the basis of their meaning. In the
primitive Indo-European language the lower numerals
were adjectives, but the words for "hundred" and
"thousand" were nouns. In English, however, as in
most of the historic Indo-European languages, the
analogy of the adjective numerals has made "hundred"
and "thousand" into adjectives. Latin *centum* is an
adjective, and so regularly is *mille*, but the plural *milia*
retained its primitive use as a noun. In this instance
association on the basis of meaning has brought about
identity of function.

Contamination is particularly common in the realm
of syntax. That is, a person often thinks of two equivalent or partially equivalent sentences and pronounces
part of each. I have frequently found myself saying,
"Why did you do that for?" and I have heard the
converse, "What did you do that?" When Plautus
(*Mil.* 619) wrote *te decora* "things worthy of you," he
had in mind the two equivalent phrases *te digna* and
tibi decora. When he wrote (*Poen.* 1308) *quid tibi hanc
digito tactiost?* he had in mind *tu hanc tangis* and *tibi
huius tactiost*. Latin *quin* "why not" was often used to
introduce a question virtually equivalent to a command;
quin dicis? "why don't you say?"=*dic* "say." A contamination of the two yields *quin dic?*, a common type
of sentence in colloquial Latin. Cicero sometimes uses
the genitive after *recordor* because that is the regular

construction after the equivalent *non obliviscor*. In the phrase *mea refert*, *mea* agrees with *re;* analogy has introduced *mea* into the equivalent phrase *mea interest*. Sometimes the contamination is between sentences that are not exactly equivalent. A combination of *Is non venit* "He did not come" with *Nullus venit* "No one came" gives us (Plautus *As.* 408) *Is nullus venit* "He didn't come at all."

It frequently happens that a sentence is summarized by a single word, such as the "fact," the "occurrence," "that," "it." Some nouns regularly serve as mere substantivized verbs, for example, "arrival," the "coming," Latin *tactio*. There are, then, many association groups which consist in part of substantives and in part of verbs or sentences; under certain circumstances the sentence "They are coming," the phrase "their arrival," and the pronouns "it," "that," etc., may be used repeatedly in a conversation with reference to the same event, that is, with identical meaning. Now, since I may say "I see their arrival," there is a tendency to substitute for the substantival phrase the semantically equivalent verbal phrase, and say "I see they are coming." In the same way such sentences as "I know it," "I know that," induce the sentence "I know they are coming." The process may be superficially described as the substitution of a sentence for a pronoun or for a substantival phrase. But psychologically it is a perfectly regular bit of analogical creation, which may be diagrammed thus: "their arrival": "I see their arrival" = "they are coming": "I see they are coming"; "it": "I know it" = "they are coming": "I know they are coming." Latin *volo eas* is due to such sentences as *volo hoc*, where the antecedent of *hoc* is *eas*.[1]   In case the antecedent of *hoc* is *ne eas*, the resulting sentence is *volo ne eas*.   Similarly, on the basis of *hoc rogatur*, *ne eas* becomes the subject of the sentence *ne eas rogatur*.

Sometimes the substitution of a sentence for a substantive leads to the development of a conjunction. In the sentence *ne eas rogatur*, *ne* is a conjunction as well as a negative adverb.   English "before" was originally a preposition, as in the sentence "I came before sunrise"; but when a sentence is substituted for the word "sunrise" ("I came before the sun rose"), "before" is a conjunction.

Many scholars suppose that such complex sentences as these have developed from a simple fusing together of two originally independent sentences: "I came before; the sun rose," and then "I came before the sun rose"; *volo; eas*, and then *volo eas*.   The difficulty with this theory is that the start-forms are scarcely credible; one would rather say, "I came; afterward the sun rose," and *eas; hoc volo*.

Nevertheless there are complex sentences whose basis is to be found in pairs of independent, or, as they are commonly called, paratactic sentences.   "I know that men are mortal" goes back to a paratactic type, such as "I know that; men are mortal."   The process by which these grammatically independent sentences

---

[1] The type may have developed in connection with some other **verb**, say, *advenias*, or with some other substantive, say, *adventum;* but the process can scarcely have been essentially different from the one sketched above.   Morris' contention (*Principles and Methods in Latin Syntax*, pp. 132 ff.) that *volo* is a mere appendage to the sentence *eas* for the purpose of emphasizing one element of that sentence, is correct enough, but it does not explain the change of function in the sentence *eas*.

came to be felt as a single sentence may be superficially described as a gradual change from parataxis
to hypotaxis. The dynamic factor, however, is the
associative interference of such simple sentences as
"I know men," "I know the mortality of men," in
which all that follows the verb is felt as the direct object.
Latin sentences, such as *vereor ne advenias*, must have
developed from the paratactic type *vereor; ne advenias*,
where *vereor* was either intransitive or elliptical for
vereor te. The *ne*-clause came to be felt as the object of
vereor through associative interference by such simple
sentences as *vereor te, vereor adventum, vereor hoc*.

Analogy based on functional association also is a
factor in syntactic change. The loss of inflectional
syllables in the English noun has left but one form to
serve as dative and accusative, that is, as indirect and
direct object; but in the masculine of the third personal
pronoun the Anglo-Saxon dative *him* and accusative *hine*
should according to phonetic law yield "him" and
*hin, respectively. The dative form has come to be
used as direct object from the analogy of the noun; the
dative "him" and all noun-forms serving for indirect
object formed a functional association group, and so
"him" acquired an additional function possessed by the
noun-forms. Latin *utor* regularly governs the ablative,
although it has come to have a sense as fully "transitive"
as that of *capio;* the inevitable association with such
verbs as *capio* gives us the accusative after *utor* in
colloquial Latin.

Just as similarity of form may assimilate the meaning
of two words, so it may assimilate their functions.
When *-ly* became the recognized termination of the

English adverbs, original adjectives, like "daily," "yearly," acquired adverbial function. We still speak of "a daily paper," but we now say also, "The paper is published *daily*." The nominative and accusative plural of neuter *o*-stems—neuters of the second declension, to use the term of Latin grammar—was originally not a plural at all, but a feminine singular with collective meaning; *templa* was a first-declension noun governing a singular verb but meaning "collection of temples." By functional analogy with genuine plurals *templa* assumed the plural inflection and came to govern a plural verb. In Greek these collective *a*-stems took the plural inflection, but continued to govern a singluar verb. Now, by the operation of phonetic laws and some analogical changes, the genuine neuter plurals of consonant stems and *i*- and *u*-stems came to have in Greek the same ending as our collectives. At that stage, of course, the whole group was associated on the basis of function (for they all designated more than one individual) and also on the basis of similarity of form. Accordingly a combination of functional and formal analogy led to the use of a singular verb with the genuine neuter plurals.

A change in the reverse direction, but resulting from the same cause, is to be seen in Latin and the Romance languages. A number of Greek neuters whose nominative singular ended in *a* were borrowed by the Romans, for example, *dogma*, *schisma*. Since they had the same ending as feminines of the first declension, they were sometimes accompanied by feminine adjectives in Latin. In Latin feminine singular and neuter plural show the same ending in the nominative, and, after final *m* was lost in late popular Latin, in the accusative too. Hence several Latin neuter plurals have become feminine singular in the Romance languages, for example, French *verve* "inspiration" from *verba; saussaie* "willow thicket" from *saliceta; esquisse* "sketch" from *schedia*.

Change of Form

Since the unit of speech is the sentence, sound-change must affect, not words, but sentences. Anglo-Saxon *ān* "one" when accented regularly became *one*, and we still retain that spelling, although the spoken language has borrowed the dialectic form *wun*, except in the compounds "only," "alone," and "atone"; but, when used without accent as the indefinite article, *ān* was not subject to the change of *ā* to *ō*, and we have *an* today (with shortening and a shift of the vowel in the direction of *e*). Such variation as this belongs to the topic of sentence phonetics. Since it differs only in detail from the types of sound-change already described, we need not discuss it further.

We must, however, notice some effects which sound-change has upon the relation of words to one another and upon the structure of the sentence. A phonetic law sometimes obliterates the distinction between two syntactic categories. Anglo-Saxon had a dative case which usually differed in form from the accusative; where Modern English has but one form, as "mouth" or "bone," Anglo-Saxon had two, for example, dative *mūðe* and *bāne*, accusative *mūð* and *bān*. The loss of final *e* made the two cases identical in form, with the result that we no longer feel any clear distinction between dative and accusative constructions, between direct and indirect object. "I give him the book" has two equally correct passives: "He is given the book" and "The book is given (to) him." Sound-change is a chief cause for the loss of inflection in the Romance languages and Modern English, and it is therefore in part responsible for the new devices which these languages use to express the relations between words. The Latin sentence *filium amat vir* cannot be translated into English in the Latin order (without a change in construction), because English has lost the original case endings of both nominative and accusative and has come to denote the relations of subject and object by means of their position in the sentence; we must place the subject before the verb and the object after: "The man loves his son." Again, the Latin phrase of two words *igne interfectus* has to be translated by a phrase of three words "killed by fire"; what Latin expresses by the ablative case English expresses by a preposition.

This same loss of inflectional syllables may leave a noun and a verb identical in form. In Anglo-Saxon there was a noun *lufu* "love" and a verb *lufie* "I love," a noun *caru* "care" and a verb *carie* "I care," a noun *help* and a verb *helpe*. In Modern English each of these pairs has yielded a single form, "love," "care," "help," which does duty both as noun and as verb. The same thing has happened to a great many other pairs, and on the analogy of these we sometimes make a verb serve as a noun without change of form, and almost any noun may serve as a verb. Thus we say not only "to pull," but also "the pull"; both "to search" and "the search"; both "to kill" and "the kill." The noun "pump" yields the verb "pump"; when we put

a man into "jail" we are said to "jail" him. The
noun "suspicion" is used by many people as a verb in
place of "suspect."

Change of Meaning—Shift of Emphasis

We have seen (pages 86 ff.) that the meaning of a
word varies considerably according to the circumstances
under which it is spoken and the character of the rest
of the sentence. This shift of emphasis from one part
of a word's signification to another very often affects
its function in the sentence. German *sehr* once meant
"sorely" and was used as an intensive in phrases similar
to the archaic English "sore wounded," "sore afraid."
Increasing emphasis upon the intensive function led to
the total loss of the original word-meaning, and so such
phrases as *sehr angenehm, sehr gut,* became possible.
The colloquial English intensives "awful" and "awfully"
are of similar origin. It requires only a slight shift of
meaning to change a noun in apposition into an adjective.
Caesar (*B.G.* vii. 20) writes *exercitum victorem* for
"victorious army." Latin *habeo* sometimes has its
ordinary meaning when followed by a perfect participle,
as in *Caesar aciem instructam habuit* "Caesar kept his
line drawn up"; but a very slight shift of emphasis
gives the meaning "had drawn up." Consequently, we
find as early as Plautus (*Ps.* 602) *illa omnia missa habeo*
"I've dropped all that." This use of *habeo* became more
common in late Latin and yielded the auxiliary verb of
French *j'ai mis*, etc. The same verb in combination
with an infinitive has yielded the French future (*scribere
habeo* became *écrirai*); the difference in meaning between
Cicero's (*Att.* ii. 22. 6) *nihil habeo scribere* and French

je n'écrirai rien is due to emphasis of the idea of futurity, which was implicit from the start.

In all the foregoing cases a loss of word-meaning has gone hand in hand with an increase of emphasis on function. In this way originate most auxiliary verbs, prepositions, and conjunctions—words whose meaning is too intangible to be accurately defined, but to which nevertheless our modern European speech owes much of its clarity and definiteness. English "around," and "away" represent an easy shift from the phrases "on round" and "on way." The Latin preposition *causa* is a case-form of a noun, and *infra* of an adjective. The English preposition "save" (Tennyson, "Who should be king save him") is in origin an imperative. English "may" develops from "He may [that is, is permitted to] go" into "It may rain."

In addition to the ordinary plural nouns most languages have a number of collective nouns which are singular in form. That Latin *multitudo*, English "crowd," etc., are virtually plurals appears from the fact that they tend to govern plural verbs, as when Shakespeare writes, "The *army* of the queen *mean* to besiege us," or when Livy writes, "*pars perexigua* . . . . *delati sunt*." "Fleet" and "ship," therefore, are identical in meaning, except for the element of number. The change from specific meaning to collective and from collective to specific involves but a shift of emphasis. The change of specific to collective is seen in English "verse" "a line of poetry" and then "poetry," as in the phrase "prose and verse." Latin *miles* means "soldier" and also "soldiery, body of soldiers," and in the same way *pedes* sometimes means "infantry" and *eques*, "cavalry." The change from collective meaning to specific is illustrated by English "youth" which, as we saw above (page 92), came to be a collective noun through the figure of synecdoche. By the process which we are now examining the collective noun "youth" ("those who are young") becomes the specific noun "youth" ("a young person") which may even make a plural "youths."

Clauses, like words, include a large number of ideas, any one of which may receive the emphasis. The clause "when the sun rises" denotes time, and also tells the circumstances under which the main statement is true. If I say, "Every day when the sun rises he is already at work," both time and circumstances are prominently expressed. In the sentence "When the sun rises, it grows light" our knowledge of the causal relation between the clauses leads us to interpret "when" as "when and because." In the sentence "When the sun rises, the valleys are still in darkness" the same knowledge leads us to feel "when" as equivalent to "when and although." In the English when-clauses the idea of time is always present, no matter how prominent any other idea may become, and accordingly we have no real change in meaning. In the since-clauses, however, the idea of time is frequently lost. In the sentence "Since the sun has risen, it is light" we may or may not think of the clause as expressing time; but in the sentence "Since the sun will rise, we prepare for work" no idea of time is possible. Concession rather than cause is the prevailing secondary meaning of the temporal sentence with "while," for example, "While then it was night, now it is day."

The so-called absolute constructions have arisen from a shift of emphasis in the meaning of a phrase. The Latin ablative absolute originally expressed accompaniment; *omnibus rebus comparatis iter fecerunt* originally meant "taking with them all the things which they had prepared, they marched." But the ablative phrase expressed situation as well as accompaniment, and with a slight shift of emphasis it came to mean "with everything prepared" (that is, everything being ready).[1]

When a phrase sinks to the position of a mark of function, that is, becomes a conjunction or a preposition, it becomes a compound word (see pages 110 f.). The locution "on account of" had reference to a column in a ledger as long as it continued to be a phrase; when it lost all concrete suggestion and came to be merely the equivalent of Latin *propter*, it became a compound word, although we still write it as three words. Since "nevertheless" has ceased to suggest negation or time or comparison, we wisely write it as one word.

A shift of emphasis is sometimes the dynamic factor in the development of a subordinate clause from a paratactic clause. The process may be illustrated by the idiomatic German sentences, such as *Es war einmal ein Mann, der hatte drei Töchter*, where *der* must be called a demonstrative and its clause paratactic, since true subordination would require the transposed order, *der drei Töchter hatte*. A somewhat better example is furnished by Homeric Greek, which does not distinguish by word-order between dependent and independent clauses: Ἀπόλλωνι ἄνακτι, τὸν ἠύκομος τέκε Λητώ, "to

---

[1] Other ablative constructions may have contributed to the ablative absolute, but the process must have been essentially the same in all cases.

Apollo the lord; him fair-haired Leto bore." No one can say whether it is better to translate the originally demonstrative τόν with "him," as we have done, or with "whom," as is customary, for the sole difference between the two is one of emphasis. In either case the antecedent of the pronoun is Ἀπόλλωνι in the main clause; if the connection between the two is felt to be relatively loose, τόν is a demonstrative; if they are felt to be closely tied together, τόν is a relative as it surely is in many passages. It is probably in about this way that demonstratives have become relatives in various languages; for example, Anglo-Saxon ðe, Sanskrit yás, Greek ὅς, Old Persian hya.

More Specific Meaning Due to a Modifier

The simplification of a phrase like "flesh meat" by the loss of one of its elements (see page 92) may involve a change of function. Latin stativus is an adjective; but stativa "permanent camp," abbreviated from the phrase stativa castra, is a noun. English "third" is an adjective, but in a phrase like "one third," where it stands for "third part," it is a noun. Here belongs the use so common in inflected languages of an adjective as a noun, for example, Latin boni, bona, perditi, sacra, Greek ῥητορική, whence English "rhetoric."

More General Meaning Due to a Pleonastic Modifier

In the primitive Indo-European language the accusative seems to have been freely used to denote end of motion, as in Latin domum it. The accusative, however, had other uses also, and the function of the case might be made clearer by an accompanying adverb of direction.

Thus (to use Latin forms in place of Indo-European) *virum eo* "to the man I go" became *virum eo ad* "to the man I go toward." In the latter sentence the relation between noun and verb is fully expressed by *ad*, and there is left for *virum* no functional force, but only the word-meaning (cf. pages 93 f.). In Latin we find the change completed for such words as *vir; ad* may no longer be omitted. Now, an interesting result of this process is its effect on the adverb of direction. As the adverb gradually usurps the functional force of the case, it comes to be felt more and more as an adjunct of the noun rather than of the verb; that is, the adverb becomes a preposition. In Indo-European and also in the earliest Sanskrit and Greek, prepositions were somewhat like the German adverb *hinauf* in *Er stieg den Berg hinauf*, while the developed prepositions of later times are more like English "up" in "he climbed up the mountain." Even in Latin such a pair of sentences as *flumen ineo* and *in flumen eo* shows that we are but one step removed from the use of *in* as an adverb; the position of the word has scarcely become fixed.

The same process weakens the personal forms of verbs until they must have a subject expressed by a separate word. Latin *respondit* meant "he replied." It was possible, however, to express a pronominal subject, such as *is* or *ille;* and the pleonasm finally deprived the verb-form of its personal force. Hence in French the expression is *il répondit*.

Figures of Speech

Metonymy often leads to a change in the relation between two words. The sentence "The cistern is running dry" is due to the use of the word "cistern" to stand for the water in it. Similarly, when we say "The river is running over," we are really talking about some of the water of the river. Sometimes the result of such a change is really nonsense, as when we say "The kettle boils." The syntactic result of the metonymy in these instances is a changed relation between the verb and its subject.

Metonymy expressed by an adjective is usually called "transferred epithet." In using the phrase "wicked ways," we do not blame the "ways" but the people who walk in them; and the result is a new relationship between the adjective "wicked" and its noun. A transferred epithet usually ascribes an attribute of personality to an inanimate object, but still without any thought of personification. Carlyle speaks of "ambitious Latin" without implying that language can feel ambition. No one imagines that a "happy event" enjoys itself, or that a "learned treatise" has studied much.

CHAPTER VII

LANGUAGE AND DIALECT

Change results in diversity. Just as the evolution of animals and plants may split one species into several, so the changes to which language is subject are constantly producing divergences in speech between persons or communities who have hitherto spoken alike. Such divergences may be of any extent, from a variation in word-meaning or pronunciation to such differences as prevent mutual understanding or even to a fundamental unlikeness of linguistic structure. The resulting varieties of speech are commonly called dialects or languages, and these terms require definition.

We usually think of a dialect as homogeneous—as a body of speech which does not contain varieties within itself—but such a definition would compel us to set up a dialect for each speaker, since the fact that we can distinguish our friends by voice proves that each one speaks in a way of his own. Furthermore, the speech of each individual varies at different times in his life, and so we should have to assume several dialects for each speaker. A more satisfactory definition is this: a dialect is a body of speech which does not contain within itself any differences that are commonly perceived as such by its users. The unity of a dialect is a unity, not of sounds produced, but of sounds perceived; it is subjective rather than objective. The only sure way, then, to determine whether or not two men use the same dialect is to appeal to the men themselves and to their neighbors. It follows that a dialect is a concrete fact. Each utterance of each speaker of the dialect is, as far as it goes, identical with the dialect itself; for by the definition the various utterances of the several speakers are not perceptibly different.

A number of dialects grouped together on the basis of certain similarities which they possess as against other dialects is called a language. A language, therefore, is an abstraction. A momentary utterance is not likely to be identical with the whole group of dialects; for, while it may contain characteristics which are common to the several dialects, it is likely to contain other elements which are peculiar to some one dialect.

Linguistic Variation

In case there is a cessation of intercourse between two parts of a linguistic community, each of the parts is subject to linguistic changes in which the other does not share, and the two resulting dialects tend to drift farther and farther apart. Such a **division of a linguistic community** most frequently results from a migration to a region that is not easily accessible from the mother-country. Pennsylvania "Dutch" differs from standard German, partly because it has been influenced by English, but chiefly because its speakers have been cut off from direct contact with Germany. When Anglo-Saxon was carried to England, it was removed entirely from the influence of the other Teutonic languages until the Danish invasions; and after the Danes ceased their inroads, contact between English and the related idioms was scarcely re-established until recent times.

Sometimes, however, the isolation of a group of speakers is incomplete; some changes spread across the border, while others are stopped. In spite of the distance between them, the separation of America from England is of this character; for numerous innovations cross the Atlantic in both directions. English "exam" has long been familiar in American schools, while "slacker" and "do one's bit" have just now been naturalized in the United States. "To make good" is an Americanism which has become current in England.

Even without any interruption of intercourse there is usually more or less linguistic **variation within a community.** In complex civilizations differences in wealth, education, and occupation always divide society into classes, and linguistic changes tend to be restricted to the class which originates them. Every trade has its peculiar slang, and every social stratum makes use of certain words, meanings, and syntactic constructions which are not approved by the next stratum above it. Not infrequently a phonetic law is confined to a class, as is the New York pronunciation of "bird" as "böid." The more sharply castes are divided, the wider the linguistic division between them is likely to be. In some savage tribes there are considerable differences between the speech of women and of men, owing chiefly to a relative isolation of the sexes. Nearly everywhere there are some differences between the speech of the old and the young, and such differences may be rather extensive.

But the isolation of classes can never be complete, even in a country where the higher classes speak a language entirely different from that of the lower classes, as was the case in England for some centuries after the

Norman conquest; for the lower classes are the servants of the higher, and the giving and receiving of orders involves linguistic intercourse. It is scarcely possible for a language to split into two mutually unintelligible class dialects, unless one of the two is an artificially fixed literary language, whose speakers employ the vernacular also.

Even where there is no interruption of intercourse within a community, many linguistic changes fail to cover the entire area. We have already discussed (page 77) the loss of *r* before a consonant which has spread from New England over New York City and a small part of New Jersey. It may ultimately cover the entire country, but, on the other hand, it may never reach far beyond its present bounds. There are many other changes which are limited to certain parts of the United States, as the southern *ah* (*ā*) for *i* (*ai*), or the use of the word "coal oil" west of the Delaware River and south of Lake Erie, whereas "kerosene" is used to the east and north.

Linguistic changes may originate at any point in a linguistic area, and each of them tends to spread outward from its point of origin. In the accompanying diagram the numbered circles indicate the territory covered by each of six linguistic changes, and the letters indicate some of the resulting varieties of speech, that is, dialects. It is evident that dialect *A* differs from dialect *l* only in that the latter has not suffered the linguistic change 5. *n* differs from *A* in the same respect and also in that it has suffered the linguistic change 3. *o* is still farther removed from *A*, since it has not shared in the linguistic change 6. *p* lacks also the change 4; it has not suffered any of the changes seen in *A*. *q* differs still more from *A*, since it has been affected by the change 1. Lastly, *B* has been still more differentiated from *A* on account of the change 2. We have then a series of intermediate dialects between *A* and *B*.

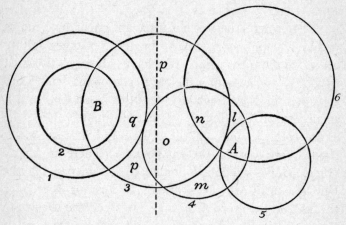

It sometimes happens that such a state of affairs is disturbed by the dying out of the intermediate dialects and the spread of the two extremes over their territory. *A* might spread over the territory of *l*, *m*, *n*, and *o*, the dialects most similar to itself, and *B* might likewise absorb *p* and *q*. The result would be two sharply distinguished dialects bordering upon each other along the dotted line. The dialects of Northern France (French dialects, properly so called) formerly shaded gradually into the Provençal dialects of the South. Today the intermediate dialects have disappeared along parts of the border, leaving French and Provençal in direct contact.

Sometimes dialectic peculiarities grow up on account of the fact that one portion of a linguistic community is influenced by another language or dialect. **Dialect mixture** of this sort occurs in three cases.

If a people speaking one language is subjugated by a people speaking another language, two languages are likely to be used in the country for some time. But finally one or the other of them gives way, not, however, without leaving traces of itself. English has driven out Norman-French, but has itself been strongly modified. Latin has supplanted the languages that were its rivals in Gaul—both Celtic and Germanic—but French shows traces of them both.

Extensive immigration of a peaceful character produces the same result more rapidly, since no feeling of hostility divides the two nationalities. This is the case with many of the foreign communities in the United States, such as the Pennsylvania "Dutch," the Swedes of Minnesota and Dakota, the Germans of Milwaukee and other cities, the Lithuanians of Chicago, the Russian Jews of New York, and many others. There is a tendency for these various groups to develop mixed dialects, not a few of which have been employed by writers of fiction, as in Myra Kelly's stories of the East Side. Still, no one of the foreign languages that has been brought into the United States is spoken by a large enough proportion of the population to enable it appreciably to modify American English. The children of foreign-born parents in America rid themselves as fully as they can, not only of their parents' native idiom, but also of the modified English which marks the first step toward naturalization. This constantly recurring process has left only a few traces, such as the loan-words "smear-case" and "kosher" and perhaps the rather extensive pronunciation of *d* and *t* for *th*.

If two linguistic areas border upon each other and no impassable natural barrier cuts off intercourse between them, most of the people along the border are familiar with both languages. They may keep the two reasonably distinct with only an occasional borrowed word, and this seems to be the usual state of affairs in civilized countries, probably because the relations with other portions of the two linguistic areas are very close. Sometimes, however, mixed dialects grow up along the border, and these are known as contact languages. Such, probably, was the origin of the Hausa language of the central Soudan, which seems to be a fusion of a language akin to the Berber dialects of North Africa, and some language or languages of the South African Bantu family.

Since dialectic variation is caused solely by linguistic changes which fail to spread over the entire community, it is clear that, if the means of communication and the habits of travel remain constant, an increase in the size of the linguistic community increases the **rate of variation.** Consequently there are more dialects in the English of the United States than in the English of British America. On the other hand, if the size of a linguistic community remains constant the possibility of dialectic variation grows less in proportion as the communication between its parts increases. There is probably less tendency toward variation in American English today than there was before the Civil War, in spite of the great increase in population.

It is no wonder, then, that among savages dialectic variation is often very great. Although the American Indians are racially similar, their languages are extremely diverse; no less than fifty-five linguistic stocks, as far from one another as Latin and Turkish, are found in North America north of Mexico, and many of these stocks contain a number of mutually unintelligible languages. In the Melanesian Archipelago every small island has its own language or even several languages. It has been estimated that the island of Celebes has hundreds of dialects. In the neighboring island of New Guinea the dialectic variety is even greater and more thoroughgoing. Shortly before their utter extinction the Tasmanians, although numbering no more than fifty persons, spoke four dialects, each with a different word for "ear," "eye," "head," and other equally common objects.

Classification of Speech

Dialects and languages may be classified on the basis of resemblances, but here, as elsewhere, this method of classification leads us into difficulty. A biologist finds that one animal resembles a second in some respects and a third in others; with which shall it be classified? So dialect A resembles dialect B in some points, but dialect C in others; how shall we decide which set of resemblances is the more important? Fortunately, we are often able to adopt a more satisfactory system. If we discover that A and B have resulted from the splitting of one earlier dialect, while C was at the earlier period quite as distinct as now, we must of course group A and B together. This genetic method of classification is usually preferred in case the history of the languages is known.

But even this method is not quite satisfactory in the case of a mixed language. If we call English a Teutonic language we are taking no account of the enormous number of Romance words which it contains. It is usual to reckon Albanian as an independent member of the Indo-European family; but its Romance element is far more important than the Romance element in English. Modern Persian is always grouped as an Indo-European language, and yet its dictionary is largely filled with Arabic words. Where shall we classify the Surinam Negro-English of Dutch Guiana, which includes English, Dutch, Spanish, Portuguese, and French? In such cases it is usual to make the commonest and most familiar words of the language the criterion. Since in English the pronouns, most of the numerals and conjunctions, and many of the most familiar nouns and verbs are Teutonic, the language itself is said to be Teutonic.

A further difficulty is caused by the spreading of linguistic changes across dialectic borders. The High German dialects owe their separation from Low German, not to a closer mutual relationship, but to certain comparatively recent changes which are common to all of them. Frankish, in fact, is partly High German and partly Low German.

Even where genetic relations are clear, there is sometimes difficulty in classification. There was once an unbroken series of dialects from Northern France to Southern Italy, with no sharp demarcation at all. The current classifications into French and Italian, or into

French, Provençal, Piedmontese, Tuscan, etc., are largely influenced by the literary dialects and political divisions.

It is of course impossible to apply a genetic classification to languages that are known only in their present form; savage languages must be classified on the basis of superficial resemblances. Even here, however, one should interpret the resemblances into genetic terms as far as possible.

The Growth of Larger Linguistic Communities

When several communities using different languages or dialects have extensive dealings with one another they feel the need of a **common language.** Unhampered intercourse is possible only in case many members of both communities speak the same idiom. Sometimes one of the natural dialects comes to serve as a common dialect, especially if its speakers are predominant in civilization or in political power. In this way the Latin dialect of Rome became the common language, first of Latium, then of Italy, and finally of large parts of Europe and Africa. On the other hand, a common language may be a mixture of elements taken from several languages. The Pidgin-English of the Chinese coast consists mainly of English and Portuguese words pronounced in the Chinese fashion and put together according to Chinese syntax. Most common languages lie between these two extremes. When the dialect of Athens became the common language of all Greeks it was somewhat modified by other dialects, especially Ionic, but it remained essentially Attic after all.

A **literary language** is a dialect that is used for literary purposes. Among the ancient Greeks many local dialects were employed in this way. In modern Europe one dialect of each language is commonly employed in literature and several others are used occasionally to get a particular effect or to supply local color. A dialect that is used only occasionally in literature is not called a literary language; even the Scotch of Robert Burns and J. M. Barrie is scarcely to be called a literary language.

A literary language tends to become a common language, and a common language tends to become a literary language. One reason why Attic Greek became the common language of the Greek world was that it had a nobler and more extensive literature than any other Greek dialect (with possibly one exception); and, when once Attic had come to be recognized as the common language, it supplanted the other literary dialects, except in certain kinds of poetry and, for a time, in the official documents of certain cities. In Luther's day several German dialects possessed a literature; but the court language of Saxony had gained some currency as a common language. For this reason Luther chose it for his translation of the Bible, and that choice in turn promoted the spread of the Saxon common language, until it is today the common language of all Germans, not only in the German Empire, but also in Austria and in Switzerland, while Danes, Norwegians, Poles, Hungarians, Russians, and others use it in order to reach a wider audience than they can by using their native languages. Chaucer chose the dialect of London because it was already beginning to be used as a common language, and Chaucer's example fixed that dialect as the common language of England. It has now become the common language of communities living in every one of the six continents and in countless islands. It may yet become the common language of the world.

A common language which has come to be used for literary purposes tends to be regarded as somehow superior to other dialects. Educated speakers prefer it to their local dialect, except when speaking to their neighbors; soon the common language is the only one taught in the schools, and presently the use of the local dialect for any purpose is a mark of boorishness. For a time after Attic Greek became the common and literary language of the Greek world, natives of Dorian cities continued to talk Doric; but as early as the time of Theocritus Doric speech was considered a mark of inferior caste in the cosmopolitan city of Alexandria. Ultimately Doric ceased to be spoken at all except in Laconia, where it survives today in the Zaconian dialect of Modern Greek.

A dialect which imposes itself upon the speakers of other dialects is called a **standard language.** The great common and literary languages of modern Europe are all standard languages. The English of London, adopted by Chaucer and most writers since his day, is taught in the schools of all Britain. The old local dialects survive, but educated people do not speak them except to a certain extent in Scotland. Even in the colonies and in America the standard language does not differ much from that of England. Until a few decades ago educated people in several parts of Germany used dialect in everyday life, although they wrote standard High German and spoke it on formal occasions; but the literary language is imposing itself with constantly increasing rigor upon ever wider and lower circles of the people. There is a similar state of affairs in France and in Italy. Greece is just starting on the same road, but the Greeks have undertaken to use instead of a local dialect an artificial compromise between the modern dialects and the ancient literary language. There is not yet perfect agreement upon the proportions of each that should be used, and until the standard language is fixed it can hardly supersede the dialects.

CHAPTER VIII

THE TREND OF LINGUISTIC DEVELOPMENT

Since language is a reflection of thought, a really perfect language is impossible until all the arts and sciences have been perfected. Dalgarno, who in 1661 invented the first artificial language, was right in trying to make his words express the exact nature of the ideas they stood for; but his classification was necessarily based upon the science of his day and would not serve us at all. In his system *de* means "element," *deb* is "fire," one of the four elements, while *deba* is "flame," the first subdivision of fire; which did very well as long as fire was thought to be an element. A language built on this principle can be permanently useful only after science and philosophy have ceased to change, although one must admit that a perfect language would have to do just what Dalgarno tried to make his language do.

Under existing conditions we can scarcely demand more of a language than that it shall represent the thought of its speakers adequately, clearly, economically, and with due regard for æsthetic effect. Even this demand is not met by any known language; and those which come nearest to the goal differ from one another in their excellences; one language is beautiful, another has a large vocabulary, and another is easy to learn.

It is not even certain that a language tends to improve in all respects with the advancing civilization of its speakers. There is no general agreement as to what constitutes æsthetic excellence in language; but, whatever

the standard, we do not find that the languages of
the most highly civilized peoples are the most beautiful,
or that languages tend to approach the standard more
closely with lapse of time. The numerous vowels of
Ancient Greek have been considered an element of
beauty; but the language contracted many of its vowels
while Greek civilization was still advancing, and Hawai-
ian has a larger proportion of vowels than the Greek
of any period. In two directions, however, a progressive
improvement of human speech may be observed;
languages tend to become more adequate and convenient
tools for the expression of thought.

Adequacy—Mental Horizon

The most obvious need of a language is that it shall
have words and syntax to express the ideas of its
speakers; the need is so imperative that probably no
language falls far behind the demands made upon it.
Some languages have small vocabularies, but their
speakers have few ideas. An unusually large vocabulary, on the other hand, does not necessarily indicate a
correspondingly great number of ideas; the huge English
dictionary is crammed with synonyms, many of which
are unfamiliar to a large part of the speakers of the language, and would be little missed if lost tomorrow. In
syntax, too, probably every language has adequate
machinery for expressing all that its users think, although
many languages are burdened with unnecessary machinery, such as grammatical gender. It is true that the
first persons who use a language for literary purposes are
likely to find the syntax troublesome and the vocabulary
quite inadequate; but the difficulty soon vanishes.

After Ennius and Plautus the Latin language was adequate for poetry of almost any type, and after Lucretius and Cicero it could easily express philosophic thought. Such an increase in adequacy results directly from a widening of the mental horizon; in so far linguistic improvement runs parallel with increase in civilization.

Analysis

The mental life of the individual begins with the mere recognition of "something there." "The baby," says James,[1] "assailed by sensations from eyes, ears, nose, skin, and entrails at once, feels it all as one great blooming, buzzing confusion." But presently the young thinker has a new experience; there is the same "blooming, buzzing confusion," but something out there—the nurse, perhaps—moves and thus gets itself isolated from the rest of the universe. Many days later humanity in general is distinguished from the great unanalyzed all, which still makes up the bulk of experience. By degrees the person-group is itself analyzed into mother, nurse, etc. Just so, as long as he lives, each individual keeps making new analyses of his experience, either of his own accord or at the suggestion of another. Occasionally an analysis is made which is new to the community as well as to the individual. There have been, in the aggregate, many such advances in the thought of mankind; upon them the development of civilization largely depends.

A new analysis which affects only the substantive parts of the stream of consciousness may be called a new idea; and the tendency to express such an idea in language does not materially differ from the tendency to

[1] *The Principles of Psychology*, I, 488.

name other discoveries. We have grouped the two phenomena together in our discussion of changes in vocabulary (pages 103 ff.).

There remains to be considered the subtler analysis which concerns also the transitive states of consciousness, that is, the distinction of function from function and of function from meaning.

Young children often use a single word or phrase for several different purposes. A child's word for "water" ("cup-a-waw," "ngink-a-waw-waw," or what not?) is, at one stage of development, used where an older person would say "Give me a drink of water" or "I've had a drink of water" or "That's a cup of water" or "Will you have a drink of water?" An older child's substitution of several sentences for the younger child's single undifferentiated phrase amounts to a discrimination between different functions. In the earlier stage "cup-a-waw" denotes a fairly definite substantive state of consciousness plus a number of transitive states of consciousness. In the second stage this group of transitive states of consciousness has been analyzed into its elements.

Although human speech has probably passed through a stage analogous to that seen in the childish "cup-a-waw," no known language even approaches such a condition. There are, however, many languages which fail to distinguish between functions which to us seem essential. In Aztec there is often no formal distinction between subject, object, and indirect object; one says virtually "he-it-him-give, it-is-king, it-is-bread, it-is-his-son" for "The king gives bread to his son."

A formal distinction between functions usually develops gradually. The Anglo-Saxon genitive was employed much as the Latin genitive to denote possession and also many other ideas; for example, *ān lȳtel sæs earm* ("a little sea's arm") "a little arm of the sea." In Modern English the genitive expresses scarcely anything but possession. In the Indo-European parent language the end of motion and the direct object seem not to have been distinguished. Even in Latin we find *Romam venit* as well as *Romam aedificat*. The former construction, however, was by that time confined within narrow limits, and in the Romance languages the discrimination between the two functions is complete. Indo-European possessed no forms which were used solely in the passive sense. In the earliest Greek the same condition persisted, since Homer sometimes employed the so-called aorist passive in a middle (that is, reflexive or intransitive) sense. In Attic Greek the aorist passive was used rather consistently in the sense which its name suggests, and in Hellenistic Greek the future passive tended to crowd out the future middle in the passive sense. In Modern Greek the old middle forms are retained, but now they regularly function as passives, except for the deponents and a few idioms. In most of the other Indo-European languages also the passive relation has within historic times become more distinct from other functions.

So far we have been discussing the distinction of function from function. There is a somewhat less widespread tendency to distinguish formally between function and meaning. Latin *Romam* in the sentence *Romam venit* expressed the same meaning as the other cases of the noun *Roma* and in addition the function of the end of motion. But, as we have just observed, the sentence

Romam venit was a survival of a type which in classical Latin was dying out. The newer type, represented by *Ad urbem venit*, denoted the function by *ad* and the meaning by *urbem*. It is true that *urbem* still continued to suggest function by its case, but in French *Il venit à Rome* the analysis is complete.

The development is, of course, not always in the same direction. While at one time the French future *j'aimerai* represented a true analysis (*aimer ai*), all speakers now feel the locution as a single word. Nevertheless most of the languages which can be studied historically show a progressive tendency toward analysis.

A characteristic difference between Latin and its modern descendants is the more analytic structure of the latter. French *j'ai aimé* analyzes Latin *amavi* into three semantic elements—two meanings and a function. French *beaucoup d'amour* (=Latin *multum amoris*) analyzes *amoris* into a meaning and a function. English shows a similar increase of analysis as compared with Anglo-Saxon. Where King Alfred wrote *Ōhthere sǣde his hlāforde* we say "Ohthere said to his lord," expressing by a preposition the function of the Anglo-Saxon dative. We translate Anglo-Saxon *dæges* "by day," *norðan* "from the north," *full wæteres* "full of water."

English has a more analytic structure than French, as may be seen by translating such French words and phrases as these: *je donne* "I give *or* do give *or* am giving," *donner* "to give," *je donnerai* "I shall give," *je donnerais* "I should give," *donnons* "let us give." It is true that in certain cases French seems to be more analytic than English, for example, *le livre de Jean* "John's book," *les bottes de sept lieues* "the seven-league boots," *de bon vin* "good wine"; but even in these examples the extra word in French is used to express three different functions, and so what is gained by the analysis of function from meaning is lost by the confusion of function with function.

Clear thinking is promoted by a relatively full analysis of thought, and the more analytic the structure of a language, the more fully must its speakers analyze their thought. It is no longer the mode to identify language with logic, and yet to a considerable extent the average man's logical attainments are due to, and limited by, his training in his native language. The following passage from John Stuart Mill's *St. Andrews Address* views the matter from an old-fashioned standpoint, but is sound in the main:

Even as mere languages, no modern European language is so valuable a discipline as those of Greece and Rome, on account of their regular and complicated structure. Consider for a moment what grammar is. It is the most elementary part of logic. It is the beginning of the analysis of the thinking process. The principles and rules of grammar are the means by which the forms of language are made to correspond with the universal forms of thought. The distinctions between the various parts of speech, between the cases of nouns, the moods and tenses of verbs, the functions of particles, are distinctions in thought, not merely in words. Single nouns and verbs express objects and events, many of which can be cognized by the senses; but the modes of putting nouns and verbs together, express the relations of objects and events, which can be cognized only by the intellect; and each mode corresponds to a different relation. The structure of every sentence is a lesson in logic. The various rules of syntax oblige us to distinguish between the subject and predicate of a proposition, between the agent, the action, and the thing acted upon; to mark when an idea is intended to modify, or qualify, or merely to unite with, some other idea; what assertions are categorical;

what only conditional; whether the intention is to express similarity or contrast, to make a plurality of assertions conjunctively or disjunctively; what portions of a sentence, though grammatically complete in themselves, are mere members or subordinate parts of the assertion made by the entire sentence. Such things form the subject-matter of universal grammar; and the languages which teach it best are those which have the most definite rules, and which provide distinct forms for the greatest number of distinctions in thought, so that, if we fail to attend precisely and accurately to any of these, we cannot avoid committing a solecism in language. In these qualities the classical languages have an incomparable superiority over every modern language, and over all languages, dead or living, which have a literature worth being generally studied.

The first sentence and the last are, as we have seen, curiously erroneous; in precisely these respects the modern European languages are superior to their predecessors. European speech has greatly improved in the last two millenniums as an instrument of exact thought and as a compelling incentive to such thought. They are more regular, not less so, and they register more, not fewer, distinctions in thought.[1]

An incidental advantage of analytic structure is the avoidance of repetition. As far as style and diction are concerned repetition is universally recognized as a fault under the name of tautology. The repetition of the expression of a function is less obtrusive, as in the phrase "a brother of mine," where the possessive idea of the pronoun is expressed also by the preposition. In "he sings and plays" the third person and singular num-

---

[1] It is quite true that study of a synthetic language by one whose native idiom is analytic has the effect which Mill claims. Even more valuable would be the study of an analytic language by one whose native idiom was synthetic.

ber are expressed by the pronoun and by each of the verbs; "he sing and play" would be a better form of expression. This sort of repetition is very common in highly inflected languages. Latin *Decurrit de superiore loco* repeats the idea expressed by *de* in the ablative *superiore* and again in the ablative *loco*. The sentence *Res erat multae operae et laboris* expresses the function of the genitive three times.

It is this sort of repetition which an analytic sentence structure avoids. The Latin sentence just cited would be rendered in English, "It was a task of much effort and toil"; the function which Latin expressed three times is expressed once for all in the preposition "of." French *de moi-même* and *de ma mère* avoid the repetition of Latin *mei ipsius* and *meae matris*, and are thus economical of effort. A brief analytic phrase, such as *de moi, j'ai aimé*, is commonly longer than the corresponding synthetic form (*mei* or *amavi*); but in connected discourse analysis makes for economy.

Association

One of the most important features of the train of thought is the tendency of certain ideas to occur together or in succession. If I think of Dr. B., I usually think of his office and then of a certain ailment to which my little son is just now subject. In some moods, however, I think of Dr. B.'s political connections and then of a certain candidate for governor of our state. Something was said above (pages 37 ff.) of this association of ideas and of its effects upon language.

Many association groups are clearly reflected in language. English "sleep," "sleeping," "sleeper," "sleepy," represent ideas which are associated on the basis of a common element, and the words themselves are tied together by similarity of form. The same statements hold with regard to "world," "world-wide," "world-weary," "worldly," "worldliness," or with regard to "sweet," "sweeter," "sweetest," "sweetness," "sweeten." In contrast to these we find other groups of associated ideas expressed by wholly dissimilar words, as "force," "dynamic," "impel," or "go," "went," "journey," "speed."

Analogy (see pages 38 ff.) tends to substitute word-groups of the first type for those of the second, as when we say "commute" and "commuter" to match "commutation," or "enthuse" to match "enthusiasm" and "enthusiast." But there are several tendencies working in the contrary direction. The association of ideas itself is so many-sided and shifting that it often creates inconcinnity; since dreams are associated with sleep, we get "dreamy" as a synonym of "sleepy," and the association of beds with sleep gives us "bedroom" beside "sleeping-room." A change of meaning frequently transfers a word to a new and incongruous association group, as when "impertinent," properly the negative of "pertinent," became a synonym of "impudent." A change of sound often makes a word less like its congeners, as when Latin *noven and *novenos became novem and nōnus. Loan-words are always a disturbing factor, except in the rare cases when a whole group of related terms is borrowed. Thus our association group "sleep," "sleeping," etc., includes such foreign words as "dormant," "somnolent," "hypnotic." Sometimes borrowed words are preferred just because their lack of associates makes them

mysterious and imposing. Religious fakirs affect such
words as "yoga," "karma," "mahātmā"; medical fakirs
prate of "psychotherapy," "hydrotherapy," "subluxa-
tion," etc. A school of dentists call themselves "ortho-
dontists" and write serious papers on the question
whether their profession shall be called "orthodontia" or
"orthodontics." Heaven forbid that it should be called
"tooth-straightening"! It is nevertheless probable that
in most languages the result of these various processes is
a net gain—a genuine tendency to assimilate the vocabulary to the association of ideas.

The tendency is much clearer, however, with regard
to the means of denoting function. In Anglo-Saxon the
plural was denoted in many different ways, as may be
seen from the following (the first word of each pair is
nominative-accusative singular and the second nominative-accusative plural): *mūð*:*mūðas*, *bān*:*bān*, *hof*:*hofu*,
spere:*speru*, *giefu*:*giefa*, *wund*:*wunda*, *hunta* (nominative
only):*huntan*, *fōt*:*fēt*, *man*:*men*, *brōðor*:*brēðer*, *frēond*:
friend. In the other cases we find very different pairs.
In the genitive, singular and plural appear thus: *mūðes*:
mūða, *bānes*:*bāna*, *giefe*:*giefa*, *huntan*:*huntena*. In the
dative sometimes the number-signs of the nominative are
reversed except for the constant dative plural ending
-um: *mūðe*:*mūðum*, *suna*:*sunum*, *huntan*:*huntum*, *fēt*:
fōtum, *men*:*mannum*. In place of this inconsistency
Modern English forms nearly all plurals with the suffix
-s, *-z*, *-iz* ("lips," "ears," "noses"), which has three
forms, to be sure, but which varies automatically, according to the preceding sound. Furthermore the Modern
English plural sign serves for all cases. The chief factor
in the simplification has been analogy. The nominative

plural ending -*as* of the *a*-stems had spread far beyond its original limits at the beginning of our records, and it has continued to spread ever since.   The present-day tendency of some speakers to say "feets" or "foots," instead of "feet," is but the continuance of this immemorial process.   The spread of the *s*-suffix to the dative plural has been due to the identical form of nominative, dative, and accusative singular which in many nouns resulted from the loss of short final vowels ("arm" [nom.]: "arm" [dat.]="arms" [nom.]: "arms" [dat.]).   The -*s* of the genitive plural is due in part to the combined influence of the other cases and in part to the influence of the genitive singular (cf. "men's," etc.).

French also shows a spread of a plural sign -*s* in place of the numerous plural signs of Latin.   The starting-point was the Latin accusative plurals in -*ās*, -*ōs*, and -*ēs*, which crowded out the neuter accusative ending -*a* and the endings of the other plural cases.   In Modern French this plural -*s*, though still written, is usually not pronounced.   In general, the sole mark of the plural of nouns is now the form of the article: *le père:les pères, l'ami:les amis.*

In the last examples the tendency toward an accurate representation of the functional association groups goes hand in hand with the tendency toward analytic structure.   The same phenomenon may be noted in several of the examples previously cited.   Latin *ad* with accusative is a more adequate expression of the function than the accusative alone, and French *à* surpasses Latin *ad* because the noun which accompanies it is free from the meaningless variation seen in the Latin accusative *urbem, oppidum, villam, turrim, mare.*

Correspondence between the association groups and the phonetically similar word-groups promotes accuracy, clearness, and vividness of speech. The sentence "This topic is impertinent" inevitably seems to most of us somehow analogous to the sentence "This child is impertinent"; our thinking is confused by the lack of correspondence between the word-group and the association group. The word "sleepy" is understood by many people who do not know the meaning of "somnolent," and the former word makes a stronger impression upon all of us—not because it is shorter or because it is "a Saxon word," but because it is phonetically similar to other words of the group.

Convenience—Regularity

The greatest advantage of the assimilation of the linguistic mechanism to the mental association groups is that this involves linguistic regularity. Plurals of English and French nouns are very much more regular in formation than Anglo-Saxon or Latin plurals. Every person who has studied both French and Latin is aware that the French declension is easier to learn than the Latin, and most of the difficulty that still remains in the French noun comes from the learning of plurals which are distinguished from the singulars in writing, although not in pronunciation. It is safe to say that French children make more rapid progress in learning to talk than Roman children did.

A still clearer example of the convenience that comes of regularity is furnished by the change of English strong verbs to weak verbs. The modern verb "help," "helped," "helped" is obviously easier to learn and to employ than Anglo-Saxon *helpan, healp, hulpon, holpen.* In Anglo-Saxon there were some 300 strong verbs, of which about 165 are still in use; but more than half of the latter number have been transferred by analogy to the regular or "weak" conjugation. Analogy may yet give us "blowed" for "blew," "knowed" for "knew," etc., with further economy of effort for every person who thereafter learns the language.

Economy

We have already seen (pages 166 f.) that analytic structure promotes the convenience of language by avoiding needless repetition. Another linguistic trait which tends to economize phonetic material is the significant word-order. We can see the beginnings of this in the older languages of our family, such as Greek and Latin. The classical writers make continual use of word-order to indicate emphasis or to point contrasts, and frequently the meaning itself is determined in this way. Greek distinguishes between ὁ σοφὸς ἀνήρ "the wise man" and ὁ ἀνὴρ σοφός "the man is wise." In Greek and Latin we can usually tell by the agreement which of several nouns an adjective modifies, but a genitive has to be assigned to its noun by the context or the word-order; for example, Horace, *Od.* i. 4. 13 f.:

> Pallida Mors aequo pulsat pede pauperum tabernas
>   Regumque turris.

We take *pauperum* and *regum* with *tabernas* and *turris* rather than with *mors* solely on account of the position. Again, the antecedent of a relative is frequently determined by the word-order; Caesar, *B.G.* ii. 24 begins:

"Eodem tempore equites nostri levisque armaturae pedites, qui cum iis una fuerant. . . . ." If word-order counted for nothing one could not decide whether to construe *qui* with *equites* or with *pedites*.

The fact remains, however, that in Greek and Latin the word-order has far less relation to the meaning than in French or English. In the Latin sentence *viri laudant Ciceronem* the relations of the words to one another are denoted by their inflectional forms. In the English sentence "The men praise Cicero" the relations of the words to one another are indicated by their order. Since the words of a sentence must be arranged in some order, it is a matter of economy to make the order significant.

It is not to be assumed, however, that a fixed word-order is necessarily advantageous. There is little to be said in favor of the inverted and transposed order of German. One of the most important improvements which English has experienced is the virtual elimination of these features of Teutonic speech. The transposed order, which may be illustrated by the Anglo-Saxon clause *siþþan hē fram his agnum hām fōr* ("after he from his own home went"), has been completely given up. We still make occasional use of the inverted order, as "There comes the man!" or "More important is our next point."

Nearly all languages show a tendency to **shorten** their **words.** The brevity of French words as compared with Latin is obvious from a glance at a page of each language. Modern English has shorter words than Anglo-Saxon. Even Modern German shows a larger proportion of monosyllables and dissyllables than the earliest remains of Teutonic speech. In Chinese and the related idioms such a tendency cannot be observed, since all their words have been monosyllables from the beginning of our records. There is some reason to believe, however, that in very ancient times Chinese had words of more than one syllable.

Other things being equal, the shorter a word the better. Long words are inconvenient because they are hard to learn and hard to remember; each time they are used they require additional time and extra effort on the part of both speaker and hearer. The Greeks and Romans called a "giraffe" *camelopardalis*. Our English word is better than this by four syllables, but a mono-syllable, such as "raf" or "gi" would be twice as con-venient as the English word. The Sanskrit word for "crown prince" is *bhavicakravartī*. Here again the Eng-lish saves four syllables, although it uses a phrase in place of a single word.

As a rule a decrease in word-length is accompanied by the development of analytic structure. The brevity of individual words, therefore, is partially compensated by an increase in the number of words; French *de moi* is no more economical than Latin *mei*. Even in this case, however, the analytic language saves effort in the end, since, as we have seen, it avoids repetition in the longer phrases *de moi-même, de ma mère*, etc.

Short words, significant word-order, and analytic structure are more or less characteristic of the modern languages of Western Europe, especially French, English, Dutch, and the Scandinavian languages. The most con-sistent exponents of all these linguistic features, however, are the monosyllabic languages of Southeastern Asia, of which Chinese is the best known. The comparative economy of languages may be statistically determined within certain limits by counting the syllables required to translate a given document.   Matthew's Gospel[1] contains in Greek about 39,000 syllables, in Latin about 37,000, in Swedish about 35,000, in German a few more than 34,000, in Anglo-Saxon about 34,000, in French about 33,000, in Danish about 32,500, in Gothic about 31,100, in English about 29,000, in Chinese about 17,000.   These figures furnish only an approximate index of the economy of the several languages, since they are in part determined by totally different factors; for example, the apparent superiority of Latin to Greek is due chiefly to its lack of a definite article and its more sparing use of conjunctive particles, neither of which features can be considered an advantage.   The unexpectedly favorable showing of Gothic may be similarly explained.   Then again, the personal equation must not be neglected; it is possible that a more skilful translator would have saved many syllables in the French version, or that a more exact translator would have added many to the Chinese version.   Still there is little doubt that in point of economy these ten languages should be arranged in about this order.

Students of language have at different times taken several different attitudes toward linguistic change. Those whose interest has been chiefly confined to some

---

[1] Part of the figures above are taken from Jespersen, *Progress in Language with Special Reference to English*, pp. 120 f., who gets some of them from Tegnér, *Språkets Makt*, pp. 51 ff.   I have estimated the Latin, German, Anglo-Saxon, and French versions by counting half the columns and multiplying the result by two.   I have counted the syllables in the 287½ extant verses of the Gothic version, and assumed the same ratio of syllables to verses for the lost portion.

one language have usually chosen a period in the history of that language as marking the climax of the excellence of the tongue—the age of Pericles, the Augustan period, the time of Elizabeth. Before that period is supposed to lie the period of growth, and after it the period of decay. The earlier comparative philologists pushed back the period of linguistic perfection for languages of our group to the time when the common ancestors of Hindoos, Persians, and Europeans dwelt together, as scholars supposed, in a sort of Garden of Eden somewhere in Central Asia. Then came a disposition to disregard the question of linguistic excellence. The business of the linguistic scholar was held to be the study of all types of language impartially; in particular, there was a protest against the disregard of popular dialects and of slang. During the last part of the nineteenth century there was a growing conviction that linguistic development is usually in the direction of improvement; and since the publication, in 1894, of Jespersen's *Progress in Language with Special Reference to English*, it has scarcely been possible to doubt that such is the case.

Can we go farther and promote the improvement of language by conscious effort? More than one system of writing has been improved to a greater or less extent by taking thought. Even our rigid but woefully illogical and inconsistent system of English orthography is largely the work of one man, Dr. Samuel Johnson; and recent efforts at a simplification of spelling have, in spite of much ridicule, made noteworthy progress. Here and there conscious effort has altered the course of development even of spoken language. If it had not been for the exertions of several generations of schoolmasters, standard English would long ago have adopted a distinction between conjunctive and disjunctive pronouns analogous to that which prevails in French—"it's me" = *c'est moi*. The constant use of a plural verb with two or more singular subjects in Modern English probably comes from the schoolroom. In the past such efforts have usually been directed against a usage that was supposed to be an innovation, but there seems to be no reason in the nature of the case why the school should not some day be enlisted in an effort to improve the language.

INDEX

INDEX

Ablaut, 118 f.

Abnormal vowels, 20

Absolute constructions, 142

Accent, 22 f.

Albanian, classification, 123, 154

Alliteration, 53

Alphabets: development, 2 ff.; imperfection, 6 ff.

Alveolars, 16

Analogical creation, 42 ff., 109 ff., 131 ff.

Analogy, 38 ff., 94 ff.; formal groups, 94 ff., 135 f.; functional groups, 40 ff., 135, 169 f.; meaning groups, 37 ff., 131 ff., 168 f.

Analysis: and association, 170; and clear thinking, 165 f.; and economy, 166 f.; of function, 162 ff.; of language, 10 ff.; of meaning, 104 f., 161 f.

Anglo-Saxon: alphabet, 8; economy, 175; genitive, 162 f.; plural nouns, 169; preterite, 49; separated from Teutonic speech, 147; word-order, 173

Anticipation, 44 ff.

Articulation: ease, 61 ff.; tendency to eliminate unfamiliar, 64 f.; unstable, 63 f.

Assimilation, 46 ff.

Association groups. *See* Analogy

Association of ideas, 37 ff.; and adequacy, 167 ff.; and analysis, 170; and clearness, 168 f., 171; reflected by form, 167 ff.; within the sentence, 44 ff.

Associative interference, 37 ff.

Auxiliary words, 138, 140, 144

Avestan vowels altered by following vowel, 48

Aztec, 162

Back-forms, 120 f.

Back-vowels, 18

Cacuminals, 16

Change in syntax, 131 ff.

Change in vocabulary, 99 ff.

Change of form: affecting several words, 68 ff.; and syntax, 137 ff.; due to associative interference, 37 ff.; due to custom, 65 f.; due to defective hearing, 33 f.; due to defective reproduction, 34 f.; due to ease of articulation, 61 ff.; due to rhythm, 56 ff.; due to speed, 60 f.; due to spelling, 65; gradual, 78 f.; gradual spread, 76 f.; irregular, 74 ff., 83 f.; isolated, 82 f.; primary, 32 ff.; regular, 69 ff., 77 ff., 83 f.; secondary, 68 ff.; sudden, 79 ff.; unknown factors, 66 f.

Change of meaning, 85 ff.; analogical, 94 ff.; and syntax, 139 ff.; due to figures of speech, 89 ff.; due to modifiers, 92 ff.; erratic, 85; shift of emphasis, 86 ff.

Chinese: accent, 59; economy, 174 f.; monosyllables, 173 f.

Classification of speech, 153 ff.

Close sounds, 17 ff.

Color-words, 107

Collectives: become plurals, 136, 140; become specific, 140 f.

Common language, 155 ff.

Composition, 110 ff.

Consonants, 15 ff.; double, 20 f.; glide after *i* or *u*, 62 f.; long, 20

Contact languages, 152

Contamination, 39, 130, 132 f.

Convenience, 171 ff.

Custom and pronunciation, 65 87 f.

PHOENIX BOOKS

PHOENIX BOOKS

PHOENIX BOOKS

 PHOENIX SCIENCE SERIES